Marketing
Your Business

John Westwood

KoganPage

LONDON PHILADELPHIA NEW DELHI

This book is for Isaac and Marissa, Jake and Isabella

First published in Great Britain and the United States in 2011 by Kogan Page Limited

120 Pentonville Road
London N1 9JN
United Kingdom
www.koganpage.com

1518 Walnut Street, Suite 1100
Philadelphia PA 19102
USA

4737/23 Ansari Road
Daryaganj
New Delhi 110002
India

© John Westwood, 2011

The right of John Westwood to be identified as the author of this work has been asserted by him in accordance with the Copyright, Designs and Patents Act 1988.

ISBN   978 0 7494 6271 0
E-ISBN   978 0 7494 6272 7

658·87
WES

British Library Cataloguing-in-Publication Data

A CIP record for this book is available from the British Library.

Library of Congress Cataloging-in-Publication Data

Westwood, John, 1947–
    Marketing your business : make the Internet work for you, get into exports, learn about products and pricing / John Westwood.
        p. cm.
    Includes index.
    ISBN 978-0-7494-6271-0 – ISBN 978-0-7494-6272-7   1. Marketing–Management.
2. Business planning.   I. Title.
    HF5415.13.W484 2011
    658.8'7–dc22
                                                                    2011002375

Typeset by Graphicraft Ltd, Hong Kong
Production managed by Jellyfish
Printed in the UK by CPI Antony Rowe

Contents

List of figures

List of tables

Introduction

To many people in business, marketing is synonymous with advertising, PR, press releases and trade shows. But marketing is much more than that. It is not the 'dark art' that many salespeople think it is. It is not just the 'ideas people' coming up with new and innovative ideas. Marketing is a science, but when you use it, it helps if you have an artistic flair. Selling is one aspect of marketing that brings in your day-to-day orders, but marketing is the tool that allows you to grow your business and to bring in orders next week, next month and next year.

In a recent interview with the *Sunday Times*, Paul Polman, chief executive of Unilever said, 'I don't see any reason why Unilever can't double in size.' Polman has put more money into marketing. He went on to say: 'If you need to restructure, you put a financial person in. If you need to grow, you put a marketing person in.'

There is much talk about a 'new marketing' for the internet age. The basic principles and theories of marketing haven't changed, but many of the tools have. Some old methods have fallen by the wayside, some have been adapted and many completely new ways of marketing your business and your products have evolved. Many of the new methods allow you to do things much more quickly and much more thoroughly than was possible even a few years ago. PR is now much more of a two-way process and advertising can be much more specific and targeted in a way that our predecessors could only have dreamt of. 'On demand printing' saves money, and online directories and e-mailshots reduce the need to print and thus do their little bit to save the planet.

The internet continues to develop and expand. It is now possible to carry out most of your market research online as 'desk research' has become 'online research'. All companies need a website and most need the facility for customers to purchase their products online. Hardware platforms are converging and internet and mobile phone technologies are converging. These changes have big implications for business.

But there are other ways of growing your business using more traditional methods combined with new technology. Application selling is a market development technique that allows companies to grow their sales by taking successful applications and promoting them in other geographical areas or in other industries. Exporting can help you to broaden your potential market, increase your turnover, improve your business's reputation, avoid being over dependent on your home sales and provide a buffer to any cyclical deterioration in the economy.

This book is not an academic textbook. It is a practical guide that will show you how to use different aspects of marketing to develop and grow your business in the internet age.

Chapter one
Marketing –
the basics

In order to use marketing to grow your business, you need to understand some of the basic principles of marketing; however that doesn't mean that you need to take a full-time marketing course. We will certainly be using marketing theory throughout the course of this book, but we will explain the theory that we need as we use it. Consider this chapter as a summary of key marketing principles and theory and refer back to it as the need arises.

How does marketing differ from selling?

The dictionary definition of marketing is: 'the provision of goods or services to meet consumer's needs'. In other words, marketing involves finding out what your customers want and matching your company's products to meet those requirements, and in the process making a profit for the company. Successful marketing involves having the right product available in the right place at the right time and making sure that the customer is aware of the product. It therefore brings in 'tomorrow's orders'.

Selling is a straightforward concept that involves persuading a customer to buy a product. It brings in 'today's orders'. It is, however, only one aspect of the marketing process.

To be successful your company must have the capability to bring in today's orders (selling) and tomorrow's orders (marketing). Most companies lose between 10 and 20 per cent of their customers each year. So if you are not planning how you can find new customers or planning for new or enhanced products to meet your existing customers' needs, you will soon be out of business.

Customers will only buy what they want. Powerful advertising is often criticized as being a tool that allows companies to persuade customers to buy what the company wants to sell. This is just not true. Two-thirds of new products fail in the marketplace. Companies have to listen to customers and the market and adapt their products. They have to become 'market-orientated'.

In many companies marketing is still considered to be more of an art than a science. Most people in sales will have been on one or several sales training courses. These courses will be selling-orientated, of the type run by organizations accredited by The Institute of Sales & Marketing Management (**www.ismm.co.uk**). As well as general courses that individual sales personnel can attend, there are also many organizations now that run excellent in-house sales training courses that are tailor-made for a particular company. They are good at teaching the basics about selling, but they teach you virtually nothing about marketing, because that is not their function. However, the same types of organization that run sales-orientated courses also run marketing courses at various levels. An introductory course on marketing can be invaluable for all sales personnel.

Even now, in large companies, the sales and marketing functions are often completely separated, sometimes with different directors for 'sales' and for 'marketing'. In some organizations, sales is a local function and marketing is handled in isolation by head office or by a 'marketing executive'. This should not be the case. The sales and marketing functions need to be combined or at least to be run with the same company aims. There needs to be a continuous interchange of information between the sales function and the marketing function.

The marketing process

Marketing is the process that brings together the abilities of a company and the requirements of its customers:

- The customers receive the benefits that satisfy their requirements.
- The company receives payment for the goods and makes some profit.

Companies have to be flexible if they want to succeed. They have to be prepared to modify or replace products as the marketplace and their customers' requirements change. They must be prepared to introduce new products or enter new markets. They must be able to read their customers and the marketplace.

A company manufacturing portable CD players in the 1990s would have had to change to manufacturing MP3 players in the last 10 years. Video player/recorders were replaced by DVD player/recorders and now these are being replaced by hard disk recorders or by downloading films from the internet. Each of these products satisfied the same basic customer need, but at a different moment in time. If the companies had not changed products, they would have gone out of business.

This balancing process takes place in the 'marketing environment', which is not controlled by individuals or by companies, is constantly changing and must be monitored continuously. There are a number of important factors that affect the way that the marketing balance is achieved in practice and affect the marketing environment.

So marketing involves:

- using the abilities of the company;
- to meet the requirements of the customer;
- in the marketing environment.

The abilities of the company can be managed by the marketing organization, which can control four main elements of a company's operation known as the 'marketing mix'. The 'marketing mix' is also often referred to as the 'four Ps'. These are four controllable variables that allow a company to come up with a policy that is profitable and satisfies its customers. They relate to:

- the product sold (Product);
- the pricing policy (Price);

- how the product is promoted (Promotion);
- methods of distribution (Place).

'Promotion' and 'Place' are concerned with reaching your potential customers in the first place, while 'Products' and 'Price' will allow you to satisfy the customers' requirements. All of these elements of the marketing mix will be covered in much greater detail in later chapters, where we will show you how to use them to best effect. But I think it would be useful to include some material here to show how these elements can be considered from a marketing perspective.

Product

The growth and decline of all products follows a life-cycle curve that can be represented as in Figure 1.1.

Ideally your company will have a portfolio of products, all at different stages in their life cycle, so that balanced growth can be achieved and risks minimized. Figure 1.2 shows a typical product portfolio.

FIGURE 1.1 Product life-cycle curve

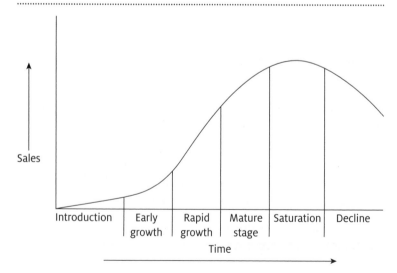

Introduction | Early growth | Rapid growth | Mature stage | Saturation | Decline

Sales

Time

FIGURE 1.2 A typical product portfolio

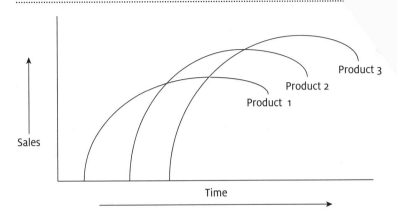

Basic types of product

From a marketing point-of-view there are three basic types of products. These are:

- consumer goods;
- industrial goods;
- services.

There are, of course, some products that could be in all three categories. Paint is an example. It can be purchased by both consumers and industrial companies and can also be part of the 'service offering' given by a house-decorating company. It is also true that not all industrial goods are capital goods and that some consumer goods such as houses or cars are capital items to the purchaser. Nevertheless, these broad definitions hold in most cases and key marketing principles apply equally to the marketing of consumer goods, capital goods and services. It is just the way that the principles are applied that takes a different form.

Consumer goods

Consumer markets are characterized by having a large number of customers. By their very nature consumer goods are usually items

ed in identical form. There are two basic types
fast-moving consumer goods and consumer

goods: sometimes called convenience
such as food, tobacco, drinks and
have a quick turnover and tend to be quickly
consumed.

- *Consumer durables*: these are items such as cars, furniture, clothing and electrical goods that are less frequent purchases and will be used by the customer for a long time.

Industrial goods

Industrial goods are any goods sold by industrial companies to manufacturers, suppliers, contractors or government agencies. The goods would normally be incorporated into other products, used within the company's own business or resold. Industrial goods can be raw materials, components or capital goods. The ultimate consumer of the final product probably has little interest in the raw materials or components used in its manufacture. Capital goods are often sold directly to the end-user – this is almost never the case with consumer goods, which are usually sold through complex distribution networks.

Services

The third basic type of product is a service. By this we do not mean the customer service that most reputable companies supply with their products, but a service as a product in its own right.

Services range from financial services such as banking and insurance to car hire and carrying out computer repairs. They differ from consumer and industrial goods in that in a service industry there is no tangible product and the product has no shelf life. Service organizations sell the benefits of their service as their product. This is an important fact that influences the way in which services are marketed.

Throughout this book, we will use examples to illustrate how various marketing tools and techniques can be used by companies selling consumer goods, services and industrial goods. For these examples we will use three fictitious companies:

- The Pure Fruit Jam Company (consumer products);
- Quality Car Hire (services);
- The Gear Pump Company (industrial products).

Price

It is generally true to say that the price level of a product will determine the demand for that product. The price that you sell your product at, and the quantity that you sell, will determine the profit you will make from these sales.

If you reduce your price you would expect to increase the demand for your product. Figure 1.3 shows a typical demand curve.

FIGURE 1.3   A typical demand curve

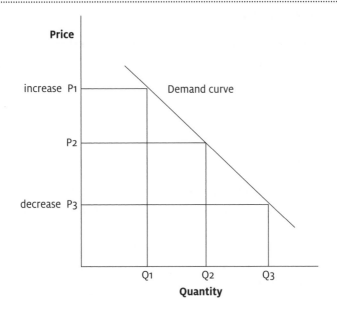

If you are currently selling your product at price P_2 and you are selling at quantity Q_2, the total value of sales is $P_2 \times Q_2$. If you increase your price to P_1, the quantity that you sell will reduce to Q_1 and if you decrease your price to P_3 the quantity that you sell will increase to Q_3. The object of the exercise is to increase the value of sales $P \times Q$ to the maximum, but to maintain P at a profitable level. If the cost of producing the items is above P_3 you cannot justify reducing your price to P_3 in the long term, because although you would sell more product it would be sold at a loss. There may, however, be good marketing reasons to justify reducing the price to P_3 or below as a short-term measure to gain market share.

We will look at products and pricing in detail in Chapter 9.

Promotion

Promotion means getting the right message across to the right people. It involves personal selling, advertising and sales promotion, all of which can be used to promote your products.

Personal selling

In an ideal world, direct selling with the salesperson face to face with the customer would give a company the maximum possibility of getting the message across and closing the sale. In the real world this is just not cost effective and all companies employ a mixture of direct and indirect sales techniques.

Advertising

The purpose of advertising is to get a message across to your customers. Advertising operates at three levels – it informs, persuades and reinforces. When it is used to inform, this normally relates to the promotion of new products and services. Advertisements intended to persuade and reinforce are what most people understand as advertising.

Sales promotion

Sales promotion is a term used to describe promotional methods using specific short-term techniques to persuade the members of the target market to respond in a particular way. The reward is something of value to those responding. This can take the form of a reduction in the price of purchasing a product or the inclusion of additional material at no extra charge.

We will look at advertising and sales promotion in Chapter 7.

Selling requires good sales-support tools. The key tools used by most companies are sales literature, presentations and exhibitions. In many companies, these are considered to be not just sales-support but sales-promotional materials. We will look at these in Chapter 8.

Place

Distribution involves selecting the right channels for your product and your business from those available. From a marketing point of view the physical distribution of goods is only one aspect of the process. Distribution involves:

- marketing channels;
- physical distribution;
- customer service.

We will look at distribution in Chapter 6.

Marketing planning

Marketing planning involves the application of marketing resources to achieve marketing objectives. It is used to segment markets, identify market position, forecast market size, and to plan viable market share within each market segment. You can use the complete process to prepare a marketing plan for your company, but you can also use the methodology to help you to set objectives for growth for a particular product or market and to generate the strategies that you need to implement to achieve them.

The marketing planning process

The marketing planning process involves:

- carrying out marketing research within and outside the company;
- looking at the company's strengths and weaknesses;
- making assumptions;
- forecasting;
- setting marketing objectives;
- generating marketing strategies;
- defining programmes;
- setting budgets;
- reviewing the results and revising the objectives, strategies or programmes.

This planning process:

- makes better use of company resources to identify marketing opportunities;
- encourages team spirit and company identity;
- helps the company to move towards achieving its corporate goals.

It can be used to:

- prepare an argument for introducing a new product;
- revamp the marketing approach for existing products;
- put together a complete company marketing plan to be included in the business plan.

It can refer to a local, national or even worldwide market. In addition, the market research carried out as part of the planning process provides a solid base of information for present and future projects.

We will use many of the techniques of marketing planning throughout this book. Some of the key ones are summarized below.

Market research

Market research can be used to look at a company's markets, customers and competitors, and also to look at the overall economic and political environment. But specifically, it can be used to collect the external and in-house information that is necessary to allow you to take informed decisions about where to commit resources to grow your business. It allows you to decide which markets have the most potential and which products are most suited to your customers' requirements.

We will look at market research in Chapter 2.

Situation analysis

Situation analysis is a process that helps you to analyse information resulting from the market research collection process and to present it in a way that you can use for planning. It can be used to:

● review the economic and business climate;
● consider where your company stands in its strategic markets and key sales areas;
● look at the strengths and weaknesses of your company – its organization, its performance and its key products;
● compare the company with its competitors;
● identify opportunities and threats.

The key process used in situation analysis is SWOT analysis. SWOT stands for:

Strengths and Weaknesses as they relate to our Opportunities and Threats in the marketplace.

The strengths and weaknesses refer to your company and its products, whereas the opportunities and threats are usually taken to be external factors over which your company has no control.

We will look at the use of SWOT analysis in Chapter 3.

Setting objectives and deciding on strategies

If you want to grow your business you need to set specific objectives. Objectives are what you want to achieve, and marketing objectives can relate to any of the following:

- selling existing products into existing markets;
- selling existing products into new markets;
- selling new products into existing markets;
- selling new products into new markets.

Marketing objectives must be definable and quantifiable so that there is an achievable target to aim towards.

Marketing strategies are the means by which marketing objectives will be achieved. It is important to understand what strategy is and how it differs from tactics. Strategies are the broad methods chosen to achieve specific objectives. They describe the means of achieving the objectives in the timescale required. They do not include the detail of the individual courses of action that will be followed on a day-to-day basis: these are tactics.

Marketing strategies relate to products, price, promotion and place.

We will also look at how you can set objectives and decide on strategies in Chapter 3.

The whole concept and process of marketing planning is covered in much more detail in my book *How to Write a Marketing Plan*, also by Kogan Page.

Summary

- Selling is a straightforward concept that involves persuading a customer to buy a product. It is only one aspect of the marketing process.
- To be successful your company must have the capability of bringing in today's orders (selling) and tomorrow's orders (marketing).

- Marketing involves using the abilities of your company to meet the requirements of your customers in the marketing environment.
- You can do this by managing the products that you sell, your pricing policy, how the products are promoted and how they are distributed.
- 'Promotion' and 'Place' (distribution) are how you reach your customers in the first place. 'Products' and 'Price' allow you to satisfy your customers' requirements.
- The principles of marketing planning can be used to help you to identify marketing opportunities. This allows you to set specific objectives and to determine the strategies that will allow you to achieve them.

Chapter two
The effective use of marketing research

Market research can be used to look at your company's markets, customers and competitors and also to look at the overall economic and political environment. But specifically, it can be used to collect the external and in-house information that is necessary to allow you to take informed decisions about where to commit resources to grow your business. It allows you to decide which markets have the most potential and which products are most suited to your customers' requirements.

You need to carry out both market research and marketing research. Market research is research about markets. Marketing research involves not just collecting information about your markets but also analysing it in the context of the marketing of your products.

Why is marketing research necessary?

In today's highly competitive business environment there is no substitute for keeping in touch with the marketplace. Markets are constantly changing and so are the requirements of customers. It is easy for a company to get so involved in one market or one sector of a market that it is not able to consider the whole market for its products and may be missing potential opportunities in other markets or market sectors.

Equally, product offerings are constantly changing and evolving in the marketplace. Competitors may have new ideas and if you do not find out about them quickly enough, you could find parts of your market starting to disappear.

Even if you do not have huge resources to commit to market research, much information is easy to get hold of if you know where to look for it. Your in-house acquired knowledge is important, as are feedback and market intelligence from your salesforce, but they need to be supplemented by market research obtained from outside sources. If you are in the consumer goods field, your contacts with the trade are unlikely to say enough about customers' attitudes and what you find out will be limited by your contacts with retailers and will not represent all views. Even if you are one of your salesforce (or *the* salesforce) your selection and interpretation of what is important will be affected by the fact that information gathering is secondary to your selling function. Although information from salespeople and other sources will be of considerable qualitative value, you need to be sure that the information on which decisions will be based is as complete as possible and is representative and objective. So additional information is required, and this would be key information relating to the companies or customers that you sell to and the industries and areas in which your product or service is being sold.

As well as information on customers, you also need information on competitors and their products. You should also obtain information about how the market and your customers perceive your company and its products. This could include company and product image, before and after-sales service, price and quality. You should research advertising and sales promotion methods to find out which are the most effective for your type of product or service.

In its simplest form the collection and evaluation process is shown in Figure 2.1.

Marketing research is used to:

- give a description of the market;
- monitor how the market changes;

FIGURE 2.1 The collection and evaluation process

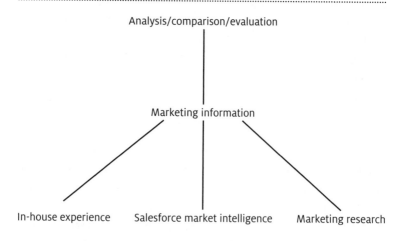

- decide on actions to be taken by a company and evaluate the results of these actions.

Description of the market

This is the primary purpose for which research is needed. It is of particular use to a company entering a market or launching a new product or service. In order to work out overall strategy, formulate the product or service correctly, and decide how to market it, it is important to learn all relevant information that is known about the products or services that are already in the market (if there are any), their market share, how they are distributed, who the users are, how frequently they use them, whether they use only one brand or several, and why they make their choices. A company entering a market would have to learn these things, but it is equally important for companies with established products to keep up to date with how and why their product is purchased.

Monitoring how the market changes

This means periodic checking for changes in a product's or brand's share or distribution, usage or image. It is dangerous to make decisions based on out-of-date information if significant changes have occurred since the original information was collected.

Deciding or evaluating potential courses of action

'Deciding on actions' relates to ways in which market research information can help a company to decide how to operate in the marketing environment. It can include the following areas:

- test marketing;
- new product launches (and developments);
- acceptance testing of modified products;
- promoting company image;
- developing and evaluating advertising and promotion campaigns, mailshots and e-mail marketing.

Methods of obtaining data for market research

Market research information consists of primary and secondary data. Primary data is obtained from primary sources: that is, directly in the marketplace. This is obtained either by carrying out field research yourself or by commissioning a consultant or market research company to carry out the fieldwork for you. Secondary data is not obtained directly from fieldwork, and market research based on secondary data sources is referred to as 'desk research'.

Small and medium-sized businesses will usually carry out limited field research themselves. Large companies in the consumer goods field may employ some of their own people for this work, but even so, most work is carried out by specialist market research companies. The sector has grown rapidly in recent years. According to Esomar (European Society for Opinion and Market Research (**www.esomar. org**), worldwide spending on market research reached $32 billion in 2008. The Market Research Society (MRS – **www.mrs.org.uk**), produces the annual survey of the UK market research industry. According to MRS, UK spending on market research in 2009 was estimated to be £2.076 billion. The UK industry has about 15,000 full-time employees with a similar number of casual or part-time workers. MRS has 6,500 members and 400 Company Partners. With members in more than 70 countries, MRS is the world's largest professional market research association representing providers and users of market research and business intelligence.

The major users of market research are the public sector, consumer goods companies and companies in IT and technology. The distribution of market research expenditure in 2009 was estimated by MRS to be as shown in Table 2.1. It can be seen that the proportion of expenditure by companies marketing industrial goods is very small compared to expenditure in the services and consumer goods sectors.

TABLE 2.1   Expenditure on market research in the UK in 2009

	Industry	%
1.	Government and public services	16.5
2.	FMCG (other than food/beverages)	16.3
3.	IT/telecommunications & consumer technology	12.0
4.	Media	9.5
5.	Business goods & services	7.8
6.	Food/beverages	7.3
7.	Financial services	7.1
8.	Non-OTC pharmaceutical and medicine	6.9
9.	Retailing (including mail order)	4.0
10.	Transport, travel and tourism	3.7
11.	Vehicles	3.1
12.	Other consumer goods and services	5.9

Field research

In field research the information is collected by obtaining the answers to a set of questions from a number of respondents. The sample used needs to be representative and objective.

Methods of carrying out field research

Field research can be carried out in person, by telephone, by post or by e-mail. Large companies often use outside companies to do the work, but small businesses usually do it themselves and limit it to just what is really necessary. Because it is an expensive process, it is best used to obtain specific information or to answer specific questions about your market. There are other methods of obtaining information in the consumer field that are part way between carrying out your own field research and desk research. These are methods such as retail audits and consumer audits.

Retail audits

The retail audit was pioneered by Nielsen in the United States. It can provide very accurate information on broad market shares, market sizes and sales trends. The principle is very simple. A representative sample of retailers is selected in a particular field (typically grocers, supermarkets, off-licences or chemists, etc). An auditor visits the retailers at regular intervals (usually twice a month). On the first visit, the auditor notes the stock of the audited items on display and in the storeroom. On the next visit the auditor notes the quantity of stock delivered since the last visit. The product sold between the visits is then calculated from the formula:

sales = initial stock + deliveries − final stock

The audit is maintained over a period of time and builds up a picture of the sales of the products and of competitive products over that time period. Setting up a retail audit is expensive and audits are normally set up to be syndicable (ie the information obtained is sold to a number of clients, most with different products). Syndication is economically possible because once the investment has been made in selecting and carrying out initial visits to the retailers, it is relatively inexpensive to collect data for a large number of products. Clients pay agreed subscriptions for packages of selected brands within a defined product field. The information is reported and presented in the way that the client requests it.

Consumer audits

Consumer audits use a panel of consumers to measure changes in attitudes or behaviour. This has the same effect as interviewing the same sample over and over again. It is either a sample of people who agreed when they were recruited that they would be available to be contacted on all sorts of subjects or, more commonly, a panel that is recruited to provide information continuously over a period. The information would need to be recorded daily otherwise it would not be remembered. So a diary is used to record purchases and consumption of particular goods. In some cases special containers are provided for used cans or cartons of the product being measured (the so-called 'dustbin check'). Consumer audits can be used to check the effect of various advertising campaigns on usage of products. They are often syndicated because of their cost.

Reactive market research with questionnaires

This is what most people associate with market research. These days it rarely involves an interviewer with a clipboard (except perhaps in an airport departure lounge). There are many ways of getting questionnaires completed. As well as personal interviews, questionnaires can also be completed through telephone interviews, as e-mail or postal questionnaires or on a company website. Nowadays it is quite common to find questionnaires in magazines, left in hotel rooms or given out in fast-food restaurants. It is a common method of gathering data because it is a flexible technique that is not necessarily very expensive, and it can be designed for statistical analysis of the questionnaires by computer. It becomes a very expensive technique if the questionnaire is badly designed so that ambiguous or inadequate data are obtained.

Questionnaires need to be specific to the area to be researched and the list of questions should be designed to give as much information as possible without ambiguity. The results can be influenced by loading questions and even the order of questions can have an effect on the answers. A questionnaire needs to be designed and set out with skill by someone with knowledge of the techniques. Even then, before it is used on a full sample, it should be pilot tested on a small section of respondents. This will highlight any problems such as ambiguous questions or omissions and the questionnaire can then be modified before being used on the full sample. More detailed guidance on questionnaire design is given later in this chapter.

The methods of getting the respondent to answer the questionnaire are compared below.

Personal interviews

This can be the most comprehensive method of carrying out field research. It allows the respondent time to ponder and to answer the questions, and it allows the interviewer the opportunity of asking additional questions or for clarification of a particular answer. It is, however, very costly in terms of both time and money. It involves travelling time and expenses as well as the actual time of the interview. There is also time required to set up the interviews.

In the consumer field the cost is increased by the need for interviewers to work unsocial hours, because with more women working and with the requirement to contact men and women in employment rather than just the unemployed, interviewing needs to be carried out in the evenings and at weekends as well as in normal daytime hours.

Nevertheless for many purposes personal face-to-face interviewing is considered an absolute necessity. A good interviewer can form a rapport with the respondents so that they focus on the subject under discussion in a relaxed and concentrated way. They can lead the respondent through the questions and can also show stimuli, such as pictures, photographs or the actual product itself – this is not possible with the other methods such as telephone and postal interviewing, although it can be done using e-mail techniques with weblinks.

Telephone interviews

Telephone interviewing is less expensive than personal interviewing because it does not incur the costs of sending interviewers out to people's homes to make the contact. People tend to be more receptive since it involves a much smaller amount of a respondent's time. This can be important in the service and industrial sector where interviews are with businessmen or engineers at work. Such people may be reluctant to agree to a personal interview because of the time involved but would rarely refuse a telephone questionnaire so long as it was not too long. Since instant answers are demanded, it is often easier to get a full set of answers from a telephone interview than from other techniques. This must be offset by the fact that instant answers are not always the answers that would be given after due reflection. In telephone interviewing the interviewer's voice is all-important, but other aspects of their personality are less important than in personal interviewing. Much greater productivity can be achieved in telephone interviewing, because there is no lost travelling time so many more interviews can be conducted in a day. There is also the facility for instant supervision and the correction of interviewer error. An additional advantage of this type of interview is that the answers can be entered directly into a computer for immediate processing.

Many companies now carry out telephone interviews when customers phone up with complaints or problems. (To encourage phone calls many companies include freephone numbers on their product packaging.) In addition to or as a means of solving the problem, a standard list of questions are asked and the answers noted. This provides the company with valuable feedback that can be analysed for reoccurring problems or trends.

Postal and e-mail questionnaires

This is a relatively low-cost method, where the questionnaire is sent by post or e-mail and the respondent is left to complete it in his or her own time. Increasingly, questionnaires are sent out with bills, supplied with new equipment or given to customers as they leave after using your service. It has the advantage, as with telephone interviewing, that it does not incur the high costs involved in sending interviewers to people's homes.

It also has a number of disadvantages:

- There is no personal contact. Because of this, it is likely that a considerable number of questionnaires will end up in waste-paper or recycle bins.
- There is no way of checking whether the person it was addressed to was really the right person to ask. Respondents can scan the whole questionnaire before they answer it and cannot be led through the questionnaire one stage at a time.
- Respondents can take as long as they wish in formulating their replies to the questions, so that postal surveys are only suitable for considered opinions and not for instant reactions.
- Response rates are often low and replies may come in over a long period of time, making it difficult to collate and analyse the results.

Most postal questionnaires are sent out with a reply-paid envelope and a reminder together with a further questionnaire is usually sent about two weeks later. E-mail questionnaires are normally also chased up with a reminder. Because of the low response rates it is important to know whether the bias of those that did not reply would affect the results of the survey. For this reason it is common to check the non-response bias by telephone calls on a subsample.

E-mailing is by far the cheapest method of sending out questionnaires. If e-mails are sent to individual persons, they can only now be sent by using an 'opt-in list'. An 'opt-in' list contains customers that have chosen to receive e-mailshots. This is now a legal requirement following a European Directive governing privacy and electronic communications. The Directive favours the 'opt-in' system and pro-hibits the sending of unsolicited electronic mail (Spam). E-mail list software is available from a number of companies. One of the most popular packages is Campaign Commander™ from Emailvision (**www.emailvision.co.uk**). A wide variety of 'opt-in' lists can be obtained from third-party e-mail list brokers. But to grow your list, you need to initiate or optimize an e-mail address collection opera-tion at all your customer points of contact (website, point-of-sale, invoices, etc).

Typical questionnaires

You will have to put together your own questionnaires based on your particular requirements, but the information given here will give you some guidelines with regard to the type of questions that you may use and the layout of the questionnaire.

Although the requirements in the consumer, service and indus-trial sectors are different, there are many factors in question-naire design that are universal. However, the content, order and layout of questionnaires will vary, depending on whether they are designed for personal or telephone interviews or for postal or e-mail questionnaires.

The following points are important:

- The questionnaire needs to be specific to the area being researched and without irrelevant questions.
- The list of questions should be designed to give as much information as possible without ambiguity.
- Each question should be simple and relatively short.
- Most questions should require a simple yes/no answer or a choice from a number of answers.
- Do not use loaded questions as these will tend to give a biased result.
- Consider the order of questions carefully, since questions earlier in the questionnaire could influence later answers.
- Lay the questionnaire out in such a way that the answers can be statistically analysed easily.

● Avoid 'omnibus' questionnaires with a hundred questions or more – most people will not be prepared to answer more than about 20 questions.

In service industries, the emphasis of questionnaires is usually on the quality of the service as perceived by the customer.

The example below shows a questionnaire prepared by Quality Car Hire. This questionnaire is on a single page that can be folded and sealed, and the resulting 'envelope' is then either left at reception or posted back to the company.

Quality Car Hire questionnaire

Date of hire: _____

Sex   male ☐   female ☐

How was our reception service on arrival?
very good ☐   good ☐   adequate ☐
   bad ☐   very bad ☐

Was the cleanliness of the vehicle:
very good ☐   good ☐   adequate ☐
   bad ☐   very bad ☐

Was the size and quality of the car:
above expectations ☐   as expected ☐
below expectations ☐

Did you find staff generally:
very helpful ☐   helpful ☐   adequate ☐
   unhelpful ☐

Would you use our services again?
yes ☐   perhaps ☐   no ☐

The Pure Fruit Jam Company is considering launching a range of specialist flavoured marmalades. It has prepared the questionnaire shown opposite. It needs to establish a number of things relating to the market. It has already obtained information on the sales levels for jams and marmalades in the UK from published data in reports prepared and sold by the Leatherhead Food Research Association. It wants to find out details about the typical consumers of marmalade. Are they male or female, young or old, how often do they purchase and where do they purchase from? This will influence the type of advertising and promotion campaign that the company will use.

The questionnaire starts with general questions relating to age and sex and then moves on to the types of marmalade and allows the company to sound out the flavours it is thinking of introducing (whisky, brandy, cointreau), as well as flavours such as vodka and gin that it thinks will have less appeal. Most questionnaires are one or two pages in length. In many cases some questions are put on the second page of a questionnaire so that the answer does not affect preceding questions.

Sometimes in the industrial goods sector, there is a requirement for more specific information that cannot be obtained by a simple yes/no answer. Also, many companies involved in industrial goods marketing are active in markets where there are only a small number of suppliers and often only a small number of customers. A supplier of consumer goods may potentially have many millions of end customers. Many industrial goods companies have fewer than a thousand active customers on their files. For this reason it is common for industrial goods companies to structure questionnaires in a more general way, mixing qualitative and quantitative types of questions. Some of the major areas that these companies often want to have their customers' or potential customers' views on are:

- buying factors that influence them;
- how they view the company and its competitors;
- how they find out about new products;
- their approach to new products.

The Gear Pump Company has prepared a number of questionnaires on these subjects.

The Pure Fruit Jam Company questionnaire

Area code: _____   Date: _____

Interview no: _____

Please complete the following information:

Sex   male ☐   female ☐

Age   10–15yrs ☐   16–20yrs ☐   21–25yrs ☐

26–30yrs ☐   31–35yrs ☐   36–40yrs ☐

41–50yrs ☐   51–64yrs ☐   65yrs and over ☐

Do you buy marmalade?   Yes ☐   No ☐

Do you buy mainly traditional Seville orange marmalade?

Yes ☐   No ☐

Do you buy specialist marmalades with other fruits or flavours?

Yes ☐   No ☐

How often do you buy marmalade?

Once a week ☐   once a month ☐   less often ☐

Do you buy from:

supermarket ☐   delicatessen ☐

by mail order ☐   other ☐

If a specialist range of marmalades was available,
which of these flavours would you be interested in?

Whisky ☐   Brandy ☐   Cointreau ☐

Sherry ☐   Vodka ☐   Gin ☐

Would you consider buying specialist marmalades:

for normal use ☐   at Christmas ☐

as a present for others ☐

Buying factors that influence customers

When you buy product A, there are a number of factors that you will take
into account in making your decision. Please list the factors given below,
numerically, in order of priority (1 to 5):

PRICE

DELIVERY

QUALITY

TECHNICAL SPECIFICATION

AFTER-SALES SERVICE

How customers view the company and its competitors

A similar questionnaire could also be used as an 'image' questionnaire to establish customers' feelings about your company. It would
include a similar list of factors, but with a different question.

Based on the buying factors listed below, how would you rate our
company?

PRICE

AVAILABILITY

QUALITY

Please rank as follows:

1 – Best on the market

2 – Better than average

3 – Average

4 – Worse than average

5 – Worst on the market

Customers' approach to new products –
How customers find out about new products

From what sources do you learn about new products in your industry? (please tick)

INTERNET

JOURNALS/MAGAZINES (PLEASE STATE WHICH ONES)

_____

_____

EXHIBITIONS (PLEASE STATE WHICH ONES)

_____

_____

MANUFACTURERS' SALES VISITS

TRADE ASSOCIATIONS

When purchasing a new product do you:

A) Contact existing users   Y/N

B) Carry out your own tests   Y/N

C) Seek other advice   Y/N (If 'yes', please specify)

_____

_____

In view of past experience, how long does it take for new products to be accepted into the industry:

A) For purchase by existing plants _____

B) For inclusion in specifications _____

Who would specify XYZ products in your company? _____

What approvals (if any) would be required? _____

Desk research

Desk research involves the collection of data from existing sources. These sources can be:

- the internet;
- ready-made reports;
- company information;
- trade directories;
- trade associations.

Desk research is much cheaper than field research and most companies only use field research when the information that they need cannot be obtained from desk research. It is clearly a waste of money to carry out your own research to obtain information that is already available and can be purchased in the form of a ready-made report. Many reports, particularly those produced by government departments or non-profit-making organizations are available free of charge. Even reports produced by commercial organizations can often be purchased for a few hundred pounds. There are of course exceptions and some industry-specific reports can cost several thousand pounds.

Before we look at how you can collect the data that you may require from the various sources that are available, we need to look at the types of data that are available.

Types of data

Market research information consists of market information and product information.

Market information

This needs to tell you:

- The market's size – How big is it?
- How is it segmented/structured?

- Its characteristics:
  - Who are the main customers?
  - Who are the main suppliers?
  - What are the main products sold?
- The state of the market:
  - Is it a new market?
  - A mature market?
  - A saturated market?
- How well are companies doing:
  - Related to the market as a whole?
  - In relation to each other?
- Channels of distribution:
  - What are they?
- Methods of communication:
  - What methods are used – Press, TV, internet, e-mail, direct mail?
  - What types of sales promotion are used?
- Financial: Are there problems caused by:
  - Taxes/duties.
  - Import restrictions.
- Legal:
  - Patent situation.
  - Product standards.
  - Legislation relating to agents.
  - Trademarks/copyright.
  - Protection of intellectual property (designs/software, etc).
- Developments:
  - What new areas of the market are developing?
  - What new products are developing?
  - Is new legislation or new regulation likely?

Product information

This relates to your potential customers, your own company and your competitors:

- Potential customers:
  - Who are they?
  - Where are they located?

- – Who are the market leaders?
- – Do they own competitors?
- Your own company:
  - – Do existing products meet customers' needs?
  - – Is product development necessary?
  - – Are completely new products required?
  - – What would be the potential of a new product?
  - – How is your company perceived in the market?
- Your competitors:
  - – Who are they?
  - – How do they compare with your company in size?
  - – Where are they located?
  - – Do they operate in the same market sectors as you?
  - – What products do they manufacture/sell?
  - – How does their pricing compare with your own?
  - – What sales/distribution channels do they use?
  - – Have they recently introduced new products?

There are four main areas of published data that can be used to provide you with market and product information. These are:

- market reports;
- company information;
- product and statistical information;
- consumer information.

These days you can carry out the bulk of desk research on the internet. General web searches will yield a wealth of information and most of the reports and other information that you will need can be obtained online and downloaded, usually as pdf files.

Market reports

Market information and market reports are the most comprehensive types of market research information. They look at all aspects of the market including companies, products, customers and trends. They present an overview of the whole market and allow a company to assess where it is positioned in the market.

The key areas covered by market reports are:

- a history of the market;
- the structure of the market;
- the size of the market;
- data on major companies in the market;
- market trends;
- distribution channels;
- recent market developments;
- future market developments.

Reports may be on a single market, a single market sector or on a number of related markets.

There are a number of companies that specialize in carrying out research and publishing reports. The most prominent are Euromonitor (**www.euromonitor.com**), Mintel (**www.mintel.co.uk**), Keynote (**www.keynote.co.uk**) and Frost and Sullivan (**www.frost.com**). These organizations publish lists of reports that they have available on their websites. Euromonitor has about 25 business reference handbooks and hundreds of reports covering 26 different industry sectors. Reports have titles as diverse as *Healthfoods in France* and *The Market for Disposable Paper Products in Asia-Pacific*. The reports include information on the market, its segmentation, the products, competition, distribution systems and the consumers. Most reports are now available in hard copy, on CD and as a pdf file that can be downloaded from the company website or received by e-mail.

There are also many specific websites for individual industries, such as **www.sugarinfo.co.uk** for the sugar industry, Leatherhead Food International (**www.lfra.co.uk**) for the food industry and Jaakko Pöyri Group (**www.poyry.com**) for the pulp and paper industry. An easy way to find out if there are any specific websites relating to your industry is to contact your trade association. Details of trade associations can be found on the website of the Trade Association Forum (**www.taforum.org**). The advantage of your trade association is that it will already have information on your industry and will be able to direct you to sites that are likely to have the information that you are looking for.

The alternative is to just use your internet search engine to carry out web searches. If you want information on the dairy industry, you could initially just type in 'dairy industry' or for the chemical industry just type in 'chemical industry'. This will bring up a long list of websites and you will certainly find that they will include companies offering reports. If it really is reports rather than general information that you require, then type in 'dairy industry reports'. If you are really only interested in the dairy industry in Europe or just the UK, just type in 'dairy industry reports + Europe' or 'dairy industry reports + UK'.

When you carry out a web search like this, you will almost certainly bring up links to information or some reports on Wikipedia (**www.wikipedia.org**). Don't immediately dismiss this out of hand. Wikipedia is a free online encyclopaedia and can be added to and edited by anyone. So you need to be cautious and check the origin and references of the material that you find. But I have found an amazing amount of useful information on Wikipedia, and in many cases it has directed me via source material to even more useful information or reports.

Government support for market research

If you need information, market or sector reports relating to overseas markets, I would suggest that before buying a report from a market research company, you contact UK Trade & Investment (UKTI). UKTI is the government organization that assists UK exporters and it has a huge amount of information and reports available on export markets. On its website (**www.ukti.gov.uk**) you can access market information on over 200 locations across the world. UKTI produces sector and market reports such as *The Aerospace Sector in India* or *The Food & Drink Sector in Brazil*. There are currently over 600 Sector and Market Reports (also called Sector Briefings and Market briefings) live on the website. These can all be accessed and downloaded as pdf files free of charge, but you need to register on the website in order to access them.

There is also an Export Marketing Research Scheme (EMRS) that is administered by the British Chambers of Commerce on behalf of UK Trade & Investment. Companies with fewer than 250 employees may be eligible for a grant of up to 50 per cent of the agreed cost of an approved marketing research project. This service helps companies carry out export marketing research on all major aspects of any export venture. This can include:

- market size and segmentation;
- regulations and legislation;
- customer needs, usage and attitudes;
- distribution channels;
- trends;
- competitor activity, strategy and performance.

You can download details of the scheme and company guidance notes from the UKTI website. You can also contact the Export Marketing Research Team at the British Chambers of Commerce directly by phone, by e-mail at emr@britishchambers.org.uk or at the website **www.britishchambers.org.uk/emrs**.

Company information

We need information on other companies in order to investigate potential customers and distributors and also to monitor our competitors and potential competitors.

Company information is of two types:

- directory information;
- financial information.

Directory information

Directory information gives key data on companies. This includes names, addresses, telephone numbers, trademarks, details of directors and who owns whom. They usually list companies operating in particular markets.

The main trade directories such as Kompass Directories (**www.kompass.co.uk**) and Kelly's Directories (**www.kellysearch.com**) cover all of the larger companies and include a great deal of information with a detailed analysis of activities and products. Kompass has a wide range of directories covering many foreign countries as well as its UK directories. There is a business-to-business search engine on its website that can be used to search its database of 2.7 million companies in more than 60 countries worldwide. Its classification system lists over 57,000 products and services in all sectors of industry and economic activity.

There are also a wide range of more specialized directories covering single industries or industry sectors (such as the chemical industry, offshore oil and gas and the textile industry). These are often not as detailed as the main trade directories and often they only show the name, address and telephone numbers of companies, with a brief list of products, but they do have the advantage of being specific to their industry. The same sort of information can also be obtained from trade associations.

In the case of a company operating locally, much useful information can be obtained from the local *Yellow Pages* (**www.yell.com**) or *Thomson Directories* (**www.thomsonlocal.com**). These companies both have online directories.

Financial information

Financial information relates to the trading performance of a company and is normally an analysis of a company's financial accounts for one or more years. By law all UK companies have to file copies of their financial accounts with Companies House. The information must include:

- the director's report and accounts;
- the annual return;
- the mortgage register;
- the memorandum and articles of association;
- changes in registered office or name;
- details of any bankruptcy proceedings.

The amount of information required from small companies is not the same as that required for large companies, and it is quite common for small companies to give no details of turnover. This can be a problem in analysing information where small companies are involved.

Copies of companies' financial accounts can be obtained by requesting a copy from Companies House (**www.companieshouse. gov.uk**). You can do this online using their WebCHeck service to find information including annual reports. These can be purchased online and downloaded as pdf files. The information given varies – small companies do not have to give turnover and divisions of larger companies may have individual reports.

More detailed information on individual companies (including financial information and credit ratings) can be obtained from specialist companies such as Dun & Bradstreet (**www.dnb.co.uk**). Whereas Companies House can only provide information on UK registered companies. Dun & Bradstreet can offer information and reports on millions of companies worldwide.

A sensible way of obtaining this kind of information for an industry is to obtain a Business Ratio Report for that industry from a company such as The Prospect Shop (**www.the-list.co.uk**) which specializes in producing such reports. These reports analyse industries by examining the results of the leading companies in the industry. The sample usually covers from 50 to 150 companies. In the reports firms are often grouped into sub-sectors in order to give a thoroughly comparative analysis. The reports include up to 25 performance ratios, such as return on capital, return on assets, profit margin and stock turnover. The companies are ranked according to ratio performance. Additionally, averages are calculated for the whole industry and where applicable each sub-sector. Information for these reports is derived from the annual audited accounts of companies filed at Companies House. In each report the tables of ratios are preceded by an informative commentary and followed by individual financial and directory profiles on all companies included in the report. The reports are available as a printed volume or in electronic format. If you want to carry out further analysis yourself, they can provide the data as comma separated (CSV) data files for easy loading into spreadsheet applications and other software.

The Prospect Shop's own database maintains detailed information on all 750,000 actively trading UK limited companies. Using this, they are able to update each title once a year at a rate of about 20–30 titles per month. They currently have over 300 reports and directories available. These reports can be useful in relating your company's performance to others in your own industry. Using the ratio approach, you can compare the performance of your company with that of major competitors.

In addition to using specialist companies to obtain financial and performance information about your competitors, you can find out a lot about them by checking out their websites. The 'Who are we' section will often give a potted history of their company and from the 'Products' section you will be able to download pdf files of their brochures and data sheets. Other information such as their mission statements, office and factory locations and details of distribution networks are also frequently available.

Product and statistical information

Government statistics are a useful source of information. These relate to business activity, as well as to details of imports and exports of products and commodities. Another useful source of international trade and production statistics is information produced by UN organizations such as the Food and Agriculture Organization (FAO). This type of information may well be irrelevant to many small businesses, but if you are involved in exporting or in the sale of industrial goods, you can find useful information to assist you. If this is not for you, please move on to the next section of this chapter.

The SIC coding system

To find your way around such statistics, it is necessary to have a basic understanding of the main coding and classification systems used for economic activity and products. There have been major changes to these systems in the last few years and, if you are looking at this type of statistics for the first time, a good guide to the development of and relationship between the systems is given in *UK Standard Industrial Classification of Economic Activities 2007* (SIC 2007). The latest updated version of this book was published in 2010 by the

Office for National Statistics, the official UK statistics organization. I would strongly recommend that you get a copy of this guide, which you can download as a pdf file free from the Office for National Statistics website (**www.ons.gov.uk**). On the website homepage, go to 'Virtual bookshelf' and then to 'Commerce, energy and industry' and then to 'Standard industrial classification' and you will find all of the free guides to SIC codings.

The SIC coding system is the one that is most commonly used by directories or financial reports to classify companies into industries by relating their main activities to the official standard industrial classification (SIC) codes. The codes in use in the UK are the SIC codes (revised 2007). (Care should be taken to differentiate these from the US SIC codes, which are different and are still in use, although they in turn are now being replaced by the NAICS system.)

The UK SIC codes are based on NACE Rev 2 (effective from 1st January 2008), which is an EU regulation requiring the use of common codes throughout the EU; where it was thought necessary or helpful a fifth digit has been added to form subclasses of the NACE Rev 2 four-digit classes. Thus the UK SIC is a hierarchical five-digit system. At the highest level of aggregation, SIC (2007) is divided into 21 sections each denoted by a single letter from A to U. These sections are given in Table 2.2.

The letters of the sections can be uniquely defined by the next breakdown, the divisions (denoted by two digits). The divisions are then broken down into groups (three digits), then into classes (four digits) and, in several cases, again into subclasses (five digits). An example is given below:

Section C	Manufacturing (comprising divisions 10–33).
Division 13	Manufacture of textiles.
Group 13.9	Manufacture of other textiles.
Class 13.93	Manufacture of carpets and rugs.
Subclass 13.93/1	Manufacture of woven or tufted carpets and rugs.

In total the SIC (2007) codings have 21 sections, 88 divisions, 272 groups, 615 classes and 191 subclasses. The codings have been expanded and changed to reflect the changes in the structure of

TABLE 2.2   Standard Industrial Classification (SIC) codings

Section	Industrial classification
A	Agriculture, forestry and fishing
B	Mining and quarrying
C	Manufacturing
D	Electricity, gas, steam and air conditioning supply
E	Water supply; sewerage, waste management and remedial activities
F	Construction
G	Wholesale and retail trade; repair of motor vehicles and motor cycles
H	Transport and storage
I	Accommodation and food service activities
J	Information and communication
K	Financial and insurance activities
L	Real estate activities
M	Professional scientific and technical activities
N	Administrative and support service activities
O	Public administration and defence; compulsory social security
P	Education
Q	Human health and social work activities
R	Arts, entertainment and recreation
S	Other service activities
T	Activities of households as employers; undifferentiated goods and services; producing activities of households for own use
U	Activities of extraterritorial organizations and bodies

industry and the new industries and products that have come into being over the last decade. In fact there have been seven reclassifications of SIC codings since they were first introduced in 1948. Although this is logical, it does mean that you have to be careful.

The result is that the SIC (2007) coding for a product will probably be different from the SIC (2003) coding, which in turn may well be different from the SIC (1992) coding. So if you are using statistical information based on SIC codes, I suggest that you confine it to recently produced information unless you are prepared to acquaint yourself with the details of the earlier versions of the system.

Both the UK SIC (2007) and the NACE Rev. 2 are completely consistent with the fourth revision of the UN's International Standard Industrial Classification of all economic activities (ISIC Rev. 4).

The Harmonized Commodity Description and Coding System

At an international level, the United Nations has the Central Product Classification (CPC), which provides a general framework for international comparisons of product statistics. The UN documentation of the CPC provides direct links to the Harmonized Commodity Description and Coding System (HS). The HS, known generally as 'tariff numbers', is the coding system used for trade worldwide.

Only the first eight digits of the HS code are of major importance. The first two digits denote the chapter, the next two digits denote the part of the chapter, the third set of two digits denotes the section and the fourth set of two digits denotes the subsection. If further digits are used, the ninth digit is a special subdivision for use in a particular country and the tenth and eleventh digits are for non-EU countries. Thus the coding HS 841360 41 0 is broken down as follows:

Chapter 84	Machinery, mech/elec appliances and parts.
Part 13	Pumps for liquids.
Section 60	Other rotary PD pumps.
Subsection 41	Gear pumps.
National 0	National breakdown (used for statistics).

The EU preferred a product classification that was more akin to the industrial activity classification, and devised the Classification of Products by Activity (CPA). One of the uses of the CPA is to code the PRODCOM lists. PRODCOM is a harmonized system used across the

European Union for the collection and publication of product statistics (it stands for 'PRODucts of the European COMmunity'). All EU countries are now using this system. The UK was the first country to start publishing statistics in May 1995. Other EU countries have followed, but not all have yet achieved the same level of coverage as the UK. The information is in the form of reports that are published annually – quarterly for some of the most popular products. The reports provide Total Market Data (UK production, or more precisely, UK manufacturer sales, exports, imports and net supply to the UK market in both value and volume terms as well as average price) on a wide range of products. The PRODCOM reports are published online by the Office for National Statistics (**www.ons.gov.uk**). The reports can be found in the same way as the SIC coding guide. Not only can you read the summaries of the reports, but you can also view or download the entire documents free of charge.

Consumer information

A considerable amount of data is available relating to consumers and consumer goods. In fact no major consumer goods company could survive for long without carrying out very specific marketing research and analysis. Such information is of value not only to companies operating in consumer markets, but also to those operating in the industrial market supplying goods to the manufacturers of consumer goods.

Consumer goods markets differ from industrial markets by having a large number of customers who are all different. Since advertising and selling on a national scale is expensive, consumer goods suppliers target sections of the market for their product.

Consumer markets are usually segmented by the characteristics of their consumers and this involves the analysis of a group of factors. Generally, consumers are classified by:

- socio-economic group;
- age;
- sex;

- occupation;
- region.

Demographic classification systems

The NRS social grades is a demographic classification system developed by the National Readership Survey in order to classify readers. It is now the most commonly used system for determining socio-economic groups in the UK. It divides consumers into six broad groups, as shown in Table 2.3.

TABLE 2.3 Consumer classification by socio-economic groups

Group	Social status
A	Upper middle class
B	Middle class
C1	Lower middle class
C2	Skilled working class
D	Working class
E	Lower class

Other classifications can be used to classify family types, housing types and area groups. These include the classification system for area of residence called ACORN (A Classification Of Residential Neighbourhoods) developed by CACI market analysis group (**www.caci.co.uk**). ACORN is a geo-demographic system categorizing all UK postcodes into various types based upon census data and other information such as lifestyle surveys. Table 2.4 shows the main ACORN categories.

Each ACORN group can be further subdivided into subgroups.

In the consumer goods industry, advertising research is also important. It is essential to know how much your competitors are spending and what they are spending it on. Advertising research can also assess which media channel is most used by customers of a given product.

TABLE 2.4 Consumer classification by ACORN groups

	Category
A	Agricultural areas
B	Modern family housing, higher incomes
C	Older housing of intermediate status
D	Older terraced housing
E	Council estates – category I
F	Council estates – category II
G	Council estates – category III
H	Mixed inner metropolitan areas
I	High-status non-family areas
J	Affluent suburban housing
K	Better-off retirement areas
L	Unclassified

How to plan your marketing research

We have now covered all of the main methods and data available for market research. Any of these methods can be used in isolation if you have a specific need for one set or type of information. But if you are carrying out more complex research, it is important to plan how you will do it to make sure that you obtain all of the information that you need. You will not need to use all of the methods and all of the types of data in every case. Figure 2.2 shows the principle of planning marketing research.

Much time, effort and cost can be wasted by starting market research projects without defining the objectives.

The key steps to carrying out the marketing research are as follows:

- Define the objectives.
- Decide what information needs to be obtained.
- Decide the best way of obtaining it.

FIGURE 2.2   Planning marketing research

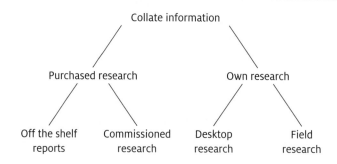

- Collect the data.
- Analyse the data.

The objectives

The objectives must be clearly defined. This should include the timescale that is necessary for completion of the work. If you sell equipment into the jam-manufacturing industry then the objective of your research would be to gather information about this industry, including its size, the major companies involved, growth patterns and so on. You should not, however, waste time gathering wider-ranging information about the food industry in general.

The information required

A list should be prepared, detailing all of the information required. This has to be a complete list of everything needed; it is extremely costly to have to go back later to collect additional information because it was not considered in the first place.

How to obtain the information

This is one of the most crucial decisions to be taken. It involves deciding who will obtain the required information and how it will be obtained. The options are:

- use own staff;
- use outside market research company;
- carry out field research;
- carry out desk research.

Only the very largest companies have market research professionals on their staff. A project involving more than a minimal amount of fieldwork is best carried out by a professional. In marketing research you get what you pay for. In practical terms large amounts of field-work are rarely necessary in the capital goods or service fields, but are quite usual in the consumer goods field.

If the requirement is for a small amount of fieldwork and a large amount of desk work, then it is usually carried out in-house. The staff chosen to do this work must be capable of understanding what they are doing. It should not be seen as just a clerical job and should only be entrusted to someone who will be able to understand the methods of marketing research and the full objectives of the project. In most small companies this task will fall to the managing director/owner or sales manager/director.

In the capital goods industries, the small amounts of fieldwork required are often carried out by the field sales staff in the course of their normal duties. The person carrying out the project will prepare a form to be completed by field sales staff based on their individual knowledge of their territory and their customers.

Collecting the data

Collecting the data involves using the methods and the data sources detailed earlier in the chapter. The names and websites for some key sources of information are listed at the end of this book in the list of useful websites.

Analysing the data

The information on its own is of no use to anyone. It needs to be verified and analysed. Verification really means being sure that the information has been collected in a logical and unbiased way.

It should be representative and needs to be as complete as possible. The assumptions used in interpreting the data need to be stated.

The analysis of the data needs to be carried out by your marketing professional. (This may be you personally.) The analysis of the data will only be as good as the understanding of the person carrying out the analysis.

Practical examples

The Pure Fruit Jam Company

The Pure Fruit Jam Company wants to find out more about the UK market for jams and marmalades. The directors know their own sales of different types of product by region of the UK, but have no idea what market share they have and how they compare with larger manufacturers.

They contact the Leatherhead Food Research Association and find that there is a report called *The UK Market for Jams, Conserves and Preserves 2003*. As non-members they can buy a copy of this for £350. From this report they can see that the UK market is estimated to be about £250 million so their share of the market is only 1 per cent. They are very small compared with the market leaders, who each sell more than £60 million. In fact in size, they are nearer to some of the specialist imported brands from France (La Belle Confiture) and Germany (Rein Konfitüre). So it becomes clear to them, that they are a niche market player.

They can also see from the regional spread of jam sales, that their major markets are the South and South West. They have weak sales in the Midlands, the North, Scotland and Northern Ireland.

They go onto Google and type in 'jam manufacturers + UK'. This search brings up the website **www.marketingfiles.com**, which is a market research company. From this site they are offered a list of the 22 jam manufacturers in the UK with details by region and county. When they purchase the list they are able to get a significant amount of information on all of these manufacturers, including turnover and main products. They also get a list of the websites of all of these companies, so that they can carry out further research on the most interesting companies.

Quality Car Hire

Quality Car Hire is a specialist car hire company that offers top of the range self-drive cars – mainly BMWs and Mercedes. They offer 'chauffeur drive' with the same cars and also with a selection of classic Rolls Royces and Bentleys. They have a leisure section that offers 'stretched limo' hire. They have offices and rental locations in Tunbridge Wells and Brighton. Quality Car Hire decide to carry out an exercise to find out the level of competition that they face. Since they are a regional company their first approach is to find out information about local companies. So first of all they contact their local Chamber of Commerce. They find that there is a trade association for car hire companies, The National Private Hire Association. From the website, they are able to get a list of car hire companies in the South East and the types of car that they rent out.

Next they look at the websites of *Yellow Pages* (**www.yell.com**) and *Thomson Directories* (**www.thomsonlocal.com**). From these sites, they are able to find details of three local companies in the Brighton area and one in Tunbridge Wells offering chauffeur-driven luxury cars and five companies offering self-drive rental. By going onto the company's websites, they are able to put together a detailed picture of their local competition.

Then they carry out a number of web searches on Google, typing in 'luxury car rental' and 'luxury car rental + Brighton'. From this they can very quickly see that their biggest competition is from large companies based in London. There are two in particular – Luxury Car Hire Ltd and Luxury Cars for Hire Ltd. They download information from these companies' websites, including pdf files of their pricing tariffs.

Finally, from carrying out further web searches they discover that the Market Research Company Ltd has produced a report entitled *The Luxury Car Rental Market in the UK*. They are able to purchase a copy of this report for £500.

The Gear Pump Company

The Gear Pump Company sets about carrying out external market research. It is looking for information on gear pumps and companies that manufacture them. For this particular exercise it is concentrating on the UK market.

It already belongs to the British Pump Manufacturers Association (BPMA). The BPMA produces company profiles of all the pump manufacturers in the UK that belong to the Association, together with details of the types of pumps that they produce. The Gear Pump Company manufacture gear pumps and from the BPMA website they can see that there are six other manufacturers of gear pumps in the BPMA. Other companies manufacture other types of pump – centrifugal, piston, diaphragm and so on.

Then they check all of their main competitors' websites. These include **www.brightpumps.com** and **www.sparpumps.com** for their main UK competitors and **www.texmanpumps.com** and **www.dvk.com** for their main overseas competitors. They also check out **www.dvk.co.uk** , which is the UK website of their German competitor DVK. From these websites they are able to download their competitors' mission statements, product literature and information about new products and other developments, such as the establishment of a new distribution centre by DVK.

Next they go to Companies House (**www.companieshouse.gov.uk**) and use the WebCHeck service to find information, including annual reports for their UK competitors. They are able to purchase the reports online and download them as pdf files. The information given varies – small companies do not have to give turnover while divisions of larger companies may have individual reports. Nevertheless a considerable number of companies still show an annual sales split between UK sales and export sales.

The next source is the Office of National Statistics (**www.ons.gov.uk**), which produces PRODCOM statistics. These are details of the value of production, imports and exports of products for the UK, using the PRODCOM headings set by Eurostat. The information is normally produced in the form of annual data publications. They type 'pumps' into the search engine on the website and it brings up a number of reports. One of the reports is entitled *Product Sales and Trade: Positive displacement pumps*. From this report they can separate out the information relating to gear pumps. By subtracting imports from exports and taking this figure from UK production, they are able to

establish that the UK market for gear pumps is £20 million. They sell
£2 million in the UK market. PRODCOM statistics also tell them that
imports are £8 million, of which £4 million come from other EU
countries.

They have now been able to establish that the UK market for their
product is about £20 million. They have sales of £2 million. Imports are
£8 million, of which £4 million come from the EU. From this data they can
produce a table showing UK market shares (see Table 2.5).

TABLE 2.5   Market share information

UK MARKET SHARE – GEAR PUMPS

Company	Turnover (£000)	Market share (%)
The Gear Pump Company	2,000	10
Bright Pumps	4,400	22
Spar Pumps	1,600	8
DVK (Germany)	3,200	16
Texman (United States)	1,600	8
Others	7,200	36

Finally the BPMA advises them that there are a number of published
reports by companies like Frost & Sullivan (**www.frost.com**) and small
market research companies. They are able to obtain a number of reports
including *Pumps and Valves in the Water Industry* and *A Survey of
Equipment Suppliers to the Food Industry.*

Summary

....

- Markets are constantly changing and so are the requirements of customers.
- A company's in-house knowledge needs to be supplemented by market research acquired from outside sources.
- The key source of market research information is the internet. Trade Associations and local Chambers of Commerce are also good sources of information on specific industries and markets.
- Market research data consists of primary and secondary data. Primary data is obtained directly in the marketplace by carrying out field research, whereas secondary data is obtained by desk research.
- Field research can be obtained by personal interviews, telephone interviews, and postal or e-mail questionnaires.
- Desk research involves the collection of data from existing sources such as government statistics, company information, trade directories, trade associations or ready-made reports.
- Market research information consists of market information and product information.
- There are a number of systems for classifying companies, products and consumer types.
- Companies can be classified by activity, using Standard Industrial Classification (SIC) codes.
- Socio-economic groupings for consumers can be classified by the NRS social grades demographic classification system or by the ACORN system for classification of residential neighbourhoods.
- All market research projects should be planned and it is important to set objectives, list the information required and decide how to obtain this information before proceeding.
- The data obtained by market research must be sensibly analysed and presented in order to make the best use of it.

Chapter three
Situation analysis

Any plan of action that you take to grow your business requires:

- establishing where you are now (situation analysis);
- deciding where you want to get to (setting objectives);
- deciding how to get there (selecting strategies and devising action plans).

This holds true whether you are planning your company budget for next year, a project to expand your sales overseas or a simple campaign to increase sales of a particular product.

In Chapter 2 we looked at the methods of carrying out market research and the types of data that are available. You can use these methods to examine your company's markets, customers and competitors as well as the overall economic and political environment that you are operating in. It addition to external market research you need to collect historical data about your company and its products. It is only when you start to analyse your own in-house data that you realize which market sectors you need to look at outside, and once you look at the external data you may notice applications that are small for your company but larger in a market context and therefore require further investigation.

Internal market research

In addition to external market research your company will have a wealth of internal data, but it is likely that much of this will not be available in the right form. You may have overall sales data, but not data itemized for individual product lines or market segments. The historical information that you need is sales/order data separated and analysed in a way that reflects the key market segments into which you sell your products.

Market segmentation

Different customers have different needs. They do not all require the same product and they do not all require the same product benefits. Even with an individual product, not all customers will buy it for the same reasons. Market segmentation allows you to consider the markets you are actually in and the markets that your company should be in.

You need to be able to split your customer base up into groups of customers who all have similar needs. Each of these groups constitutes a market segment.

For consumer goods and services, it is usual to classify the end-users by the use of methods of classification that separate consumers by socio-economic group, age, sex, occupation or region.

The marketing of industrial goods and services is different, because the customer is usually another company or a government department. The number of customers is therefore more likely to be 10 thousand than 10 million and could be only a few hundred in the case of suppliers to power stations, coal mines and the like. The main ways of defining segments here are by:

- geographical area;
- industry or industry sub-sector;
- product;
- application;
- size of end-user;
- distribution channel – distributor, equipment manufacturer, end-user.

Segmentation can also be based on:

- order size;
- order frequency;
- type of decision-maker.

The key to market segmentation is to let the marketplace segment itself, because the individual segments, whether they be socio-economic groups, geographical areas or industries, exist independently of the company and its products.

For the products and markets you are looking at, you should collect information going back two or three full years together with the current year's historical sales. You should show margin information relating to those sales, where it is available. You should also adjust figures for inflation and have them available in their actual and adjusted forms.

Information checklists

Before you start collecting internal data, it is useful to prepare an information checklist. The exact content will vary, but it should include details of the segmentation that you want for sales, the split of your customer base, and competitor activity/market shares. The detail of the information will vary, depending on the type of company and this will mean that detail listed in the checklist will also vary and should be customized to your company.

Examples of checklists

The Pure Fruit Jam Company

1. Sales history

The last three years' sales by value (including margins where available) for:

- Sales areas UK: South, North, Wales, Scotland/NI.
- Sales areas (export): North America, Europe, Japan, Australia.

- Product groups: standard jams, marmalades, mini-pots, gift packs.

- Markets: supermarkets, quality shops, hotels, airlines.

Also unit sales:

- number of standard jars – by product;

- number of mini-pots – by product;

- number of gift packs.

2. Customers

Total number of customers by:

- Sales areas UK: South, North, Wales, Scotland/NI.

- Sales areas (export): North America, Europe, Japan, Australia.

- Products bought: standard jams, marmalades, mini-pots, gift packs.

- Market: supermarkets, quality shops, hotels, airlines.

- Key customers: top 40 by sales turnover.

3. Competition

- Who are the competitors for each product group?

- What are the market shares for each product for each competitor?

Quality Car Hire

1. Sales history

The last three years' sales by value (including margins where available) for:

- Sales areas: Sussex, Kent, Surrey, Greater London.

- Product groups: prestige car self-drive, prestige car with driver, classic luxury car with driver, stretched limo with driver.

- Markets: standard car hire, business, leisure, travel.

Also unit sales:

- number of self-drive car hires by car size/type;

- number of chauffeur-driven car hires by car size/type.

2. Customers

Total number of customers by:

- Sales area: Sussex, Kent, Surrey, Greater London.

- Products bought: prestige car self-drive, prestige car with driver, classic luxury car with driver, stretched limo with driver.

- Market: standard car hire, business, leisure, travel.

- Key customers: top 40 by sales turnover.

3. Competition

- Who are the competitors for each product group?

The Gear Pump Company

1. Sales history

The last three years' sales by value (including margins where available) for:

- Sales areas – South, Midlands, North, Wales, Scotland/NI.

- Product groups – industrial gear pumps, micro gear pumps, gear sub-assemblies, packages.

- Main equipment and spares.

Also unit sales:

- number of pumps by model size;

- number of packages by model size.

2. Customers

Total number of customers by:

- Sales area: South, Midlands, North, Wales, Scotland/NI.

- Products bought: industrial gear pumps, micro gear pumps, gear sub-assemblies, packages.

- Market: chemical/petrochemical, water treatment, paper, food.

- Key customers: top 40 by sales turnover.

3. Competition

- Who are the competitors for each product group?

- What are the market shares for each product for each competitor?

How to present the information

The sales data can be split up into separate tables geographically, by product, by industry or under all of these categories.

The figures can be easily prepared on computer spreadsheets such as Microsoft's Excel or Lotus SmartSuite's 1–2–3. These programs have the facility for the data entered into the spreadsheet tables to be displayed graphically as well.

Below we give some examples of how the sales figures could be presented for our sample companies.

The Pure Fruit Jam Company splits its sales into UK and export sales. In Table 3.1 we show its UK sales by product group.

It is important to it to know how many jars of jam it sells as well as the value of sales. Table 3.2 show its unit sales for jam products in the UK.

For Quality Car Hire the number of individual hires of different types of car is also important. This is shown in Table 3.3.

TABLE 3.1   Sales figures for UK (all products)

THE PURE FRUIT JAM COMPANY

SALES FIGURES

SALES AREA: UK

YEAR (all values in £k)	20X3	20X4	20X5
STANDARD JAMS (340gm)	1,000	1,000	1,000
MARMALADES (340gm)	350	350	420
MINI-POTS	100	180	250
GIFT PACKS	90	70	50
SPECIAL PRODUCTS	150	200	280
TOTAL	1,690	1,800	2,000

TABLE 3.2   Unit sales of jam products for the UK

THE PURE FRUIT JAM COMPANY

SALES FIGURES

SALES AREA: UK

YEAR (000s of jars/packs)	20X3	20X4	20X5
STANDARD JAMS (340gm)	1,100	1,130	1,160
MARMALADES (340gm)	290	265	325
MINI-POTS	400	700	950
GIFT PACKS	47	33	25
SPECIAL PRODUCTS	80	105	140
TOTAL	1,917	2,233	2,600

TABLE 3.3 Individual car hires by product per year

QUALITY CAR HIRE

SALES FIGURES

SALES AREA: ALL

YEAR	20X3	20X4	20X5
No of hires			
PRESTIGE CAR (self-drive)	18,500	17,220	18,570
PRESTIGE CAR (with driver)	3,125	2,750	3,080
CLASSIC LUXURY (with driver)	1,020	1,528	1,890
STRETCHED LIMO (with driver)	310	580	972
TOTAL	22,955	22,078	24,512

The Gear Pump Company decides to look at the sales of its individual products in each of its UK sales regions. Table 3.4 shows sales of its range of industrial gear pumps. It produces similar tables for each of its other product ranges.

TABLE 3.4 Sales of a product by region

THE GEAR PUMP COMPANY

SALES FIGURES

SALES AREA: UK

PRODUCT: INDUSTRIAL GEAR PUMPS

YEAR (all values in £k)	20X3	20X4	20X5
SOUTH	295	250	230
MIDLANDS	485	415	360
NORTH	525	420	300
WALES	45	55	60
SCOTLAND/NI	50	60	50
TOTAL UK	1,400	1,200	1,000

Situation analysis

Completing your market research and collecting historical data about your company and its products is the first step. You then need to analyse this information so that you can use it for planning purposes.

Situation analysis is a process that helps you to do this. It can be used for any of the following:

- to review the economic and business climate;
- to consider where your company stands in its strategic markets and key sales areas;
- to look at the strengths and weaknesses of your company – its organization, its performance and its key products;
- to compare your company with its competitors;
- to identify your opportunities and any threats to your business.

SWOT analysis

The key process used in situation analysis is SWOT analysis. SWOT stands for:

> Strengths and Weaknesses as they relate to our Opportunities and Threats in the marketplace.

The strengths and weaknesses refer to your company and its products whereas the opportunities and threats are usually taken to be external factors over which your company has no control. SWOT analysis involves understanding and analysing your strengths and weaknesses and identifying threats to your business as well as opportunities in the marketplace. You can then attempt to exploit your strengths, overcome your weaknesses, grasp your opportunities and defend yourself against threats. SWOT analysis asks the questions that will enable you to decide whether your company and products are really up to the job and what the constraints will be.

In carrying out SWOT analysis it is usual to list the strengths, weaknesses, opportunities and threats on the same page. This is done by segmenting the page into four squares and entering strengths

and weaknesses in the top squares and opportunities and threats in
the bottom squares as shown in Table 3.5.

TABLE 3.5   Presentation of SWOT analysis

STRENGTHS	WEAKNESSES
....	....
....	....
....	....
....	....
....	....

OPPORTUNITIES	THREATS
....	....
....	....
....	....
....	....
....	....

You can use SWOT analysis to look at any aspect of your company, its
products and markets. You can prepare a SWOT on your company, its
organization, your main competitors, your products, your geographical
sales areas or your key market segments.

The *strengths* of a company and its organization could be such
things as:

- For a large company:
  - It is well known in the marketplace.
  - It has good resources.
- For a small company:
  - It could be more flexible.
  - All customers are personally known.
- It has a good sales organization.
- It has a good distribution network.

- The company has a low-cost manufacturing base in China.
- It has a 'quality' image.

Weaknesses could be such things as:

- Competitors are larger and well known in the marketplace.
- The company has an inadequate sales organization.
- It is difficult to recruit qualified staff locally.
- It has a bad image for 'quality' or for 'on-time delivery'.
- The company has an inadequate or non-existent distributor network.
- It has an inadequate or non-existent service network.
- It has only one manufacturing centre and this is in an area with high labour costs.
- Its competitors have a better or more complete distributor network.

Opportunities could be such things as:

- The company has been taken over by a company that is a large potential customer for its products.
- The company has recently been merged with another company, giving it the advantage of economies of scale in manufacturing.
- Recent investment has given the company an edge over its competitors.

Threats could be such things as:

- Its largest customer has recently taken over one of its major competitors.
- Short-term exchange rate changes are reducing the company's profit margins on overseas business.
- A foreign competitor is building a new factory in the UK.
- A new product from a major competitor has made one of its key products obsolete.

Examples of SWOT analyses

Some examples of SWOT analyses are shown in Tables 3.6 to 3.11:

TABLE 3.6 Company SWOT for The Pure Fruit Jam Company

STRENGTHS	WEAKNESSES
We have a quality image	Our advertising spend is small compared with major players
We have good resources – financial and technical	We are still not well known in major European markets
We are known for our use of fresh fruits and natural ingredients	Our export distribution is weak

OPPORTUNITIES	THREATS
To grow sales in export markets	Well-known European brands benefit from economies of scale
To develop new products	Weakening US dollar would affect sales growth in the United States
To further reduce costs	

TABLE 3.7 Quality Car Hire – SWOT for a product: classic luxury cars with driver

STRENGTHS	WEAKNESSES
Good range of products: classic Rolls Royce and Bentleys	Even second-hand, each car costs £50k–£100k
The product enthuses luxury	High running costs
	We need a high usage rate to make a profit

OPPORTUNITIES	THREATS
Add specialist large old American cars (50s/60s type)	If competitors move into this product it could start a price war

TABLE 3.8 The Gear Pump Company – SWOT for a market segment: water treatment

STRENGTHS	WEAKNESSES
A market we all know well	A 'lowest price' market
Our products are well known and respected in the industry	
We have industry experts	
OPPORTUNITIES	THREATS
New investment programme to meet EU directives	No longer 'buy British' bias
Our components now sourced in Far East	Some water companies now owned by foreign companies (French/German/US)

TABLE 3.9 The Gear Pump Company – SWOT for a product: micro gear pumps

STRENGTHS	WEAKNESSES
Available in 304 or 316 stainless steels	High cost/high price
Good range of sizes	The product is not yet well established in the water industry
Well established with OEMs	
OPPORTUNITIES	THREATS
Reduce costs by using castings	Cheap imports from Asia
Use as 'metering product'	Competing products in special plastics
Add control package	

TABLE 3.10   The Pure Fruit Jam Company – market segment: quality shops

STRENGTHS	WEAKNESSES
High-price 'prestige' market	Limited number of shops
They have all-year-round and not just seasonal clientele	Need to contact a lot of individual buyers
OPPORTUNITIES	THREATS
Mail order and Christmas catalogues for big-name shops	All our competitors target them too
	These specialist shops reduce in numbers every year

TABLE 3.11   The Pure Fruit Jam Company – SWOT for a competitor: Rein Konfitüre

THEIR STRENGTHS	THEIR WEAKNESSES
Large company	They lack local coverage in the UK
Part of an international group	Old-fashioned flavours (raspberry, strawberry, blackcurrant)
They have a good name	
OPPORTUNITIES FOR US	THREATS TO US
High value of the euro	They may set up their own company in the UK
Our new flavours	They may buy a UK producer

Once you have carried out a situation analysis you will be ready to move on to setting your objectives and deciding your strategies.

Setting marketing objectives

Objectives are what you want to achieve; strategies are how you get there. A marketing objective concerns the balance between products and their markets. It relates to which products you want to sell into which markets. The means of achieving these objectives, using price, promotion and distribution, are marketing strategies. There will then be tactics and action plans – all to enable you to achieve your objectives.

Marketing objectives relate to any of the following:

- selling existing products into existing markets;
- selling existing products into new markets;
- selling new products into existing markets;
- selling new products into new markets.

Marketing objectives must be definable and quantifiable so that there is an achievable target to aim towards. 'Achievable' is the key word. An objective that is clearly impossible to achieve will be seen as a disincentive by your sales team. Marketing objectives should be defined in such a way that actual performance can be compared with the objective. They should be expressed in terms of values or market shares, and vague terms such as increase, improve or maximize should not be used.

The following are examples of marketing objectives:

- to increase sales of the product in the UK by 10 per cent per annum in real terms, each year for the next three years;
- to increase market share for the product from 10 per cent to 15 per cent over two years;
- to increase sales of the product by 30 per cent in real terms within five years.

You need to have short-term as well as long-term objectives. Increasing sales by 30 per cent over five years may seem a huge rise, but if you redefine it as increasing sales by 5 or 6 per cent a year, it will appear to be much more achievable.

You may set some marketing objectives based on opportunities identified in your SWOT analyses. You may have already decided that you want to develop your sales of a particular product in a specific market segment – which could be geographical or by industry. You may be developing your export business and putting together a programme for developing sales in a particular country. Or you may be launching a new product into your established markets.

Examples

The Pure Fruit Jam Company

The Pure Fruit Jam Company is launching some new ranges of flavoured breakfast marmalades in the UK. It has set as its objective:

- to increase annual sales of marmalades in the UK from £420,000 to £600,000 within three years.

Within that objective it has a number of sub-objectives including:

- to grow sales of rum-flavoured marmalade from zero to £60,000 within three years.

It is also planning to develop its sales in Japan, and for that it has set a number of objectives:

- to grow sales in Japan from £50,000 to £300,000 within three years;
- to increase our sales of mini-pots to hotels from £20,000 to £100,000 within three years;
- to gain £50,000 a year of sales of mini-pots to airlines within three years;
- to increase sales to quality shops/supermarkets to £150,000 within three years;
- to grow sales of gift packs from £30,000 to £90,000 within three years;
- to sell £60,000 a year of specialist marmalades in Japan within three years.

Quality Car Hire

Quality Car Hire is planning to grow its stretched limo service and has set itself the objective:

- to grow annual turnover of stretched limo hire from £136,000 to £180,000 within two years.

It is also intending to add large old American classic cars to its range and intends:

- to generate an additional £100,000 of annual turnover by the year 20X8 from a new range of American classic cars.

The Gear Pump Company

The Gear Pump Company is planning to increase its sales into the water industry. It intends to:

- increase our sales into the water industry by 20 per cent within three years.

In order to achieve this it intends to:

- increase sales of industrial gear pumps into the water industry by 32 per cent within three years;
- grow sales of micro gear pumps and packages into the water industry to £300,000 within three years.

It is also improving its distribution in Scotland and Northern Ireland. The objective here is to:

- double distributor sales in Scotland and Northern Ireland by the year 20X8.

Marketing strategies

Once you have set your objectives you need to consider how they can be achieved. The way that you go about achieving your marketing objectives is through marketing strategies.

It is important to understand what strategy is and how it differs from tactics. Strategies are the broad methods chosen to achieve specific objectives. They describe the means of achieving the objectives in the timescale required. They do not include the detail of the individual courses of action that will be followed on a day-by-day or month-by-month basis. These are tactics. So a strategy is the broad definition of how the objective is to be achieved, the action steps are tactics and the action plans contain the detail of the individual actions, their timing and who will carry them out. A decision to 'market price' a product is a strategy, but the decisions to decrease prices by a certain percentage in one market and to increase by a certain amount in another are tactics.

Marketing strategies relate to products, pricing, advertising/promotion and distribution. They do of course also relate to selling, but selling is usually included under the heading of 'promotion'.

Marketing strategies relate to general policies for the following:

- Products:
  - changing product portfolio/mix;
  - dropping, adding or modifying products;
  - changing design, quality or performance;
  - consolidating/standardizing.
- Price:
  - changing price, terms or conditions for particular product groups in particular market segments;
  - skimming policies;
  - penetration policies;
  - discount policies.
- Promotion:
  - changing selling/salesforce organization;
  - changing advertising or sales promotion;
  - changing public relations policy;
  - increasing/decreasing exhibition coverage.
- Distribution:
  - changing channels;
  - improving service.

For any project there will undoubtedly be many strategies that could be used, so you need to narrow these down by considering only those strategies that offer the greatest chance of success. All of the strategies should be consistent with each other and with the objectives that they are expected to achieve.

Types of strategy

One way of looking at strategies is to consider whether they are defensive, developing or attacking. All strategies are one of these types or a combination of more than one.

Defensive strategies

These are designed to prevent loss of existing customers.

Your SWOT analyses will have highlighted a number of 'weaknesses'. These could relate to your company, its organization, the products or service offered. Strategies can be designed to overcome these weaknesses and to consolidate your company's position in the marketplace.

If one weakness was that a company had a bad reputation for quality, the logical strategy would be 'to improve quality'. If the product was considered to be old-fashioned, the necessary strategy could be to repackage (for a consumer product) or re-engineer (for an industrial product).

Typical defensive strategies would be:

- improve company image;
- improve quality/reliability of product/service;
- improve reliability of delivery promises;
- restyle/repackage product/service;
- improve performance of product;
- improve durability of product;
- overcome product faults.

Developing strategies

These are designed to offer existing customers a wider range of your products or services. These strategies are based on modifying products or introducing new products to your existing customers in your existing markets. From your SWOT analyses, you will have identified a number of 'opportunities' that can be exploited. Some of these will relate to the market's requirements and how they are being fulfilled by your existing product or product range. If you have a range of four sizes of product, you may have identified a market requirement for another size of the product larger than your largest unit, or smaller than your smallest size. Examples of this are the introduction of bags of 'mini-bars' by chocolate companies and paint in bulk size containers in DIY stores.

The introduction of such products can often offer the simplest and least risky strategy to increase turnover. Typical developing strategies would be:

- increase range of sizes/colours/materials offered;
- increase range of services offered;
- increase range of extra features/options;
- find different uses for product;
- develop new product;
- make product more environmentally friendly.

Attacking strategies

These are designed to generate business through new customers. This type of strategy involves finding new customers for your product in your existing markets or new customers in new markets. No company has a 100 per cent coverage of its existing market and new customers can be found or attracted from competitors by offering better quality, price or service. Also, new customers can be found in new geographical or industry market segments. Typical attacking strategies would be:

- change pricing policy;
- use new sales channels;

FIGURE 3.1 Ansoff matrix: the risks of various strategies

		LOW RISK	HIGH RISK
		Present product	New product
LOW RISK	Present market	Expand existing market with existing product	Develop new products for existing markets
HIGH RISK	New market	Sell present product in new markets	Develop or acquire new products to sell into new markets

- find new distribution outlets;
- enter new geographical markets;
- enter new industry sectors.

A useful way of looking at the types of strategy that may be available is to use a matrix that was developed by Ansoff, as shown in Figure 3.1.

It can be seen from this matrix that the least risky way to try to expand your business is in the areas you know best – ie with your existing products in your existing markets.

A higher-risk strategy is to sell existing products into new markets, which involves the development of market entry strategies. At least with this type of strategy there is only one unknown – the new market – and you are selling something that you know you have sold successfully in your existing markets.

To develop new products for existing markets is an even more risky strategy, but one that most companies have to try at some time or another. If an existing product is reaching the end of its life cycle there will be no choice but to use a strategy of this type. Many companies have a continuing strategy of introducing one new product every few years to spread the risks.

To develop or acquire new products to sell into new markets is the most risky strategy of all and should not be attempted if other options are available.

Devising strategies

Strategies can come from many different sources and it is wise to consider all possible ways of generating potential strategies. Some may seem to follow logically and obviously from the objectives, but others may evolve in a flash of inspiration. When the list of alternative strategies has been prepared, they should be evaluated to determine which will best satisfy the objectives. You should also determine which strategies can be best implemented with the resources and capabilities that your company has.

Strategies should be listed under the headings of the four main elements of the marketing mix – product, pricing, promotion and distribution. Examples of specific marketing strategies are shown in Chapter 9 (product and pricing), Chapter 7 (promotion) and Chapter 6 (distribution), together with some of the tactics that could be employed.

Examples

Earlier in this chapter we looked at some of the objectives for our sample companies. Now we can look at the strategies that they have chosen to help them achieve these objectives.

The Pure Fruit Jam Company set as its objective for launching some new ranges of flavoured breakfast marmalades in the UK:

- to increase annual sales of marmalades in the UK from £420,000 to £600,000 within three years.

It has decided to adopt the following set of strategies:

Product

- Launch rum and cointreau-flavoured marmalade.
- Launch new-look gift packs.

Pricing

- Offer retrospective discount to major outlets based on level of annual purchases.

Promotion

- Carry out high-profile product launch for rum and cointreau-flavoured marmalades.

Distribution

- Expand outlets in major cities in North and Scotland.

- Sell mini-pots through Hotel Catering Services Ltd.

- Expand website to allow online purchases.

We also saw that it is planning to develop its sales in Japan and the overall objective that it has set is:

- to grow sales in Japan from £50,000 to £300,000 within three years.

The following is the list of strategies that it is adopting to help it achieve this:

Product

- Repackage gift packs for the Japanese market – information in Japanese, but retain 'British quality feel'.

- Add sake-flavoured marmalade to range.

Pricing

- Premium-price alcohol-flavoured marmalades – particularly whisky and brandy.

Promotion

- Use government grant to produce Japanese sales literature.

- Take part in Nippon Food Show in Osaka as part of the British Pavilion, using government grant support.

Distribution

- Use British Embassy – commercial section to help find representative in Osaka (for west of Japan).

One of Quality Car Hire's objectives is:

- to generate an additional £100,000 of annual turnover by the year 20X8 from a new range of American Classic cars.

Its chosen strategies are:

Product

- Buy two large American classic design 1950s/60s cars – one saloon and one open top convertible.

Pricing

- Premium price at 20 per cent above the current pricing structure for stretched limos.

Promotion

- Photo and video clip on website.

- E-mailshot to existing users of stretched limo service.

- Flyers in tourist information bureaux in Brighton, Eastbourne, Hastings and Tunbridge Wells.

Distribution

- Use our existing distribution.

- Subcontract through Luxury Car Hire Ltd for the London area.

One of the objectives of The Gear Pump Company in terms of developing its water industry sales is:

- Grow sales of micro gear pumps and packages into the water industry to £300,000 within three years.

Its chosen strategies are:

Product

- Put new cast version into production by March 20X6.

- Add 'Egro' control unit and package as a metering pump system for polymer dosing.

Pricing

- Offer discount structure to key contractors.

Promotion

- Mailshot/e-mailshot to water companies and water treatment contractors.

- Take part in Iwex exhibition at NEC.

Distribution

- Increase sales coverage by recruiting salesman for the water industry.

Action plans

Once you have selected the outline strategies and tactics to achieve your marketing objectives, you need to turn these strategies into programmes or action plans that will enable you to give clear instructions to your staff. If you will be carrying out the work yourself, you still need a clear listing of the actions and timescale to work to.

Each action plan should include:

- *Current position* – where you are now.
- *Aims* – what to do/where you want to go.
- *Action* – what you need to do to get there.
- *Person responsible* – who will do it.
- *Start date*.
- *Finish date*.
- *Budgeted cost*.

Each action plan would need to be broken down into its component parts.

Examples

The Pure Fruit Jam Company

The Pure Fruit Jam Company is preparing an action plan for the product launch of its new range of specialist marmalades. This is shown in Table 3.12.

TABLE 3.12 An action plan for The Pure Fruit Jam Company for its UK product launch

ACTION PLAN – Product launch for specialist marmalades

DEPARTMENT: SALES & MARKETING

Aim	Action	By	Start	Finish	Cost
Carry out product launch	Prepare launch package	JAW	1.1.X6	1.6.X6	£5,000
	Manufacture samples	AKH	1.3.X6	15.5.X6	£3,000
	Book venues and hotels	EBG	1.11.X5	1.1.X6	£8,000
	Book stand design and build	JAW	1.1.X6	1.6.X6	£13,000
	Commission launch video	JAW	1.1.X6	1.6.X6	£10,000
	Book advertising	EBG	1.3.X6	1.4.X6	£15,000
	Send out invitations	EBG	1.3.X6	1.4.X6	£300

This action plan is only a summary of the key overall tasks. 'Prepare launch package' is in itself a complex job with a number of constituent parts that all have to be produced before the launch:

● press release;
● leaflet;
● launch video;
● letter to key customers;
● letter to distributors;
● press advert;
● jam 'kits' – including a sample of each jam.

Similarly, 'booking venues' involves booking venues for an internal company launch, press launch, a launch to key customers and a launch to key distributors. 'Send out invitations' also includes actions to update the list of who should be invited – from the press, from customers and from distributors.

The company also prepares an action plan for producing a Japanese brochure for the export initiative that it is making into Japan. This is shown in Table 3.13. This plan does not show one single order with the agency, because payments are made on completion of individual parts of the work.

TABLE 3.13   An action plan for the preparation of a Japanese brochure by The Pure Fruit Jam Company

ACTION PLAN – Produce Japanese brochure

DEPARTMENT: SALES

Aim	Action	By	Start	Finish	Cost
Produce Japanese brochure	Meet with agency for kick-off meeting	AHF/IGT	15.1.X6	15.1.X6	£200
	Prepare text – UK text with changes for Japanese market	IGT	15.1.X6	28.2.X6	£100
	Get text translated at Nippo	IGT	28.2.X6	22.3.X6	£850
	Get photography done	AHF	1.2.X6	1.3.X6	£800
	Check initial artwork	AHF/IGT	1.3.X6	1.4.X6	£500
	Check final artwork	AHF/IGT	15.4.X6	30.4.X6	£2,500
	Print	AHF	15.5.X6	30.5.X6	£2,500

Quality Car Hire

Quality Car Hire is planning to expand its website to take orders online and also to add 'web analytics' software for e-marketing. This system will allow it to analyse hits on the site and help it to prepare its own lists of who visits the site and the products they are interested in. The action plan is shown in Table 3.14. This is just the initial action plan. When the order is placed with the supplier, a schedule of the work together with key dates must be prepared by the supplier. This should tie in with the dates that have been shown in the action plan above.

TABLE 3.14 Action plan for expanding website

ACTION PLAN – Expand website to take orders and add 'web analytics' software for e-marketing.

DEPARTMENT: SALES

Aim	Action	By	Start	Finish	Cost
Expand website to take orders on-line and add 'web analytics' software for e-marketing	Select company to carry out work	DFL	1.1.X6	1.3.X6	£200
	Place order	DFL	1.3.X6	1.3.X6	£8,000
	Test site	DFL/NAF	1.4.X6	1.6.X6	£2,000
	Go live	NAF	1.6.X6		

The Gear Pump Company

The Gear Pump Company is taking part in the IWEX water treatment exhibition in November 20X6. Their action plan for this is shown in Table 3.15. To get a good position they have to book their stand a year ahead. They also have to book hotels well in advance to avoid being too far away from the exhibition site. Most of the actions shown on the action plan will again be broken down into a list of sub-actions with dates and responsibilities.

TABLE 3.15   An action plan for exhibition participation

ACTION PLAN – IWEX exhibition

DEPARTMENT: SALES

Aim	Action	By	Start	Finish	Cost
Exhibit at IWEX	Book exhibition stand	BNK	1.11.X5	1.11.X5	£8,000
	Place order for stand design and build	ANT	1.2.X6	1.3.X6	£10,000
	Agree artwork	BNK	1.6.X6	1.6.X6	£5,000
	Book hotels	ANT	1.2.X6	1.2.X6	£2,000
	Book carpets, furniture, lighting	BNK	1.6.X6	1.6.X6	£3,000
	Final approval meeting	BNK	1.7.X6	1.7.X6	

Summary

- Any plan of action that you take to help grow your business requires establishing where you are now (situation analysis), deciding where you want to get to (setting objectives) and deciding how to get there (selecting strategies and devising action plans).
- Your company is a valuable source of data and your own historical 'in-house' data should be added to the more general market information collected by external market research.
- You need to be able to split your customer base up into groups of customers who have similar needs. Each of these groups constitutes a market segment.

- Before you start collecting internal data, it is useful to prepare an information checklist.
- The information should be collected and presented in such a way as to reflect the key market segments into which you sell your products.
- You need to analyse this information using situation analysis to help you to clearly understand the current position of your company and its products in the marketplace.
- Marketing objectives must be definable and quantifiable and should be expressed in terms of values or market shares. They should be a challenge, but should be achievable. They should be motivating rather than discouraging.
- Marketing strategies are the methods by which you achieve your marketing objectives. The individual courses of action that are followed on a day-to-day basis are tactics.
- Strategies must be converted into programmes or action plans so that they can be carried out. Each action plan should include details of your current position, the aims, the actions to be taken, who is responsible for each action, when each action should start and when it should be completed, together with the budgeted costs.
- Each department and member of staff needs to know their responsibilities and the timetable for carrying them out.

Chapter four
Websites and
e-commerce

The internet is a global system of interconnected computer networks that use the standard Internet Protocol Suite (TCP/IP) to serve billions of users worldwide. But practically the internet is just about the most important tool that you can use to help you grow your business.

It seems amazing that it was only in August 1991 that the world wide web project was first publicized and only 1994 when Netscape released the first commercial browser, Netscape 1.0. The first e-commerce site was also set up in 1994 by Pizza Hut in California offering online ordering of pizzas on its web page! The growth has been phenomenal. According to the International Telecommunications Union (ITU), by 2002 about 10 per cent of the world's population used the internet and this had grown to about a quarter of the world's population by 2010.

Internet vs web

The terms internet and world wide web are often used in everyday speech without much distinction, but they are not the same thing. The internet is a global communications system. It is the hardware and software infrastructure that provides connectivity between computers. In contrast the web is one of the services communicated via the internet. It is a collection of interconnected documents and other resources, linked by hyperlinks and URLs (Uniform Resource Locator: this is the standard way an address is presented on the internet. The first part indicates what protocol to use and the second part specifies the domain name, eg '**mycompany.com**'.)

The internet is a powerful tool that you should use to the full. That doesn't necessarily mean that you will eventually be making all of your sales online through your website, although with some businesses that may be the case. From carrying out market research to doing e-mailshots, the internet is providing more and more ways of growing your business in a cost-effective way. This doesn't mean that all the older methods of promoting and distributing your products are now dead, but it does mean that you have powerful additional methods at your disposal.

Websites

The internet provides a major sales channel for all types of products. Most companies of any size have online purchasing. Major supermarket chains now encourage online purchasing and customers can order their weekly shopping online and have it delivered to their door. Hotel rooms and packaged holidays can also be booked online, either directly with the hotel/package-tour provider, or at specialist sites such as **www.expedia.co.uk**. Books and CDs can be purchased from a number of sites including **www.amazon.co.uk**. Computers, cars, electrical goods can all be ordered online.

One effect of these websites is to drive down prices, because the consumer can now surf the web and compare prices from different suppliers. Even consumers who like to view major items before they purchase them can go into their local store, select the product that they want and then check if they can purchase it more cheaply via the internet (which they probably can). On many websites consumers can also read what other people thought of the product they are thinking of purchasing. Sites such as Amazon have customer ratings and customer testimonials for most products.

But there is an additional advantage to companies in terms of getting the best out of their websites and in using them for sales promotion. The use of web analytics software means that companies can now track which pages of their website are most popular, which promotions are clicked on most – basically which parts seem to attract users and which parts don't. They can track where users enter and where they leave, where they come from (which search engines, etc) and where they go next, how long they stay on the site and how many pages they look at while they are there. This is far more detailed feedback than is available in other media.

Most industrial companies now also use their website to provide information on their products and to publicize new products and sales successes. The advantage of a website is that even small companies can give the impression of being large and knowledgeable. In addition to company websites, there are now also a range of independent websites for specific types of industrial equipment (pumps and valves, vacuum equipment, mixing equipment) or industries (pulp and paper, chemical manufacturing, water and waste treatment).

Setting up a website

There are a number of steps to setting up a website for your company:

1 Choose and register a domain name.
2 Choose a company to host your website.
3 Design your website or choose a company to do it for you.

Domain names

Your domain name is the title and address of your website. Most website owners try to buy a domain name that says something about their business or what their site does, or one that incorporates their main brand or company name.

A domain name is the first part of the web address after www. that is entered into a web browser to find a web page on the internet. (It is also the part after the @ sign in an e-mail address.) So in the web address **www.mycompany.com**, 'mycompany' is the domain name. The second part of the address, '.com', is called the TLD (Top Level Domain). There are different types of TLD:

- Generic top level domains (gTLD), eg '.com' or 'gov' – these are typically used for organizations.

- Country code top level domains (ccTLD), eg '.uk' for the UK or '.de' for Germany.
- Unsponsored top level domains (uTLD), eg '.biz' or '.info' that are used for various services.

In addition, the registration of domains with the '.co' TLD opened in July 2010.

The choice of TLD is really a matter of personal preference. '.com' is seen as being more international and '.co.uk' is seen as being UK only. The TLD '.eu' for European Union is also common, rather than using a country code. For a UK company I would recommend trying to purchase the same domain name with both '.com' and '.co.uk' and possibly also '.eu'.

In June 2010 the Internet Corporation for Assigned Names and Numbers (ICANN) met in Brussels to finalize the application process and timetable for the liberalization of domain names, with a whole raft of new TLDs being made available for use from 2012. With the liberalization of domain names, almost any TLD from '.airlines' to '.zulu' will be made available, but they will be sold to the highest bidder. Someone winning the bid for '.airlines' would be able to sell variants of the suffix, such as easyjet.airlines or japan.airlines to the relevant companies.

When you are looking for a domain name for your company website, remember that the most popular names will have already been taken, so you may have to compromise. The cost of registering a domain name is not high, probably no more than £30 a year for a '.co.uk' domain name. (It can be free if you register it through your web hosting company.) So if they are available it can be a good idea to register several types of domain name, since it stops other people registering them and leaves them ready to use either straight away or in the future. When you register a domain name, it is usually registered for an initial period of either one or two years. If you forget to renew it, you will lose it, which would be a costly mistake. The advantage of registering it through your web hosting company is that they will automatically advise you when it is coming up for renewal and renew the registration for you for a further registration period. Equally, if you decide you no longer want to use a particular domain name, you can just let it lapse.

In selecting a domain name there are a number of other things to consider:

- Not all domain names will be available – you may have to compromise. So if **www.motors.com** is not available you may have to settle for **www.motors.co.uk**, **www.ukmotors.com** or **www.motorsuk.com**.
- If you are an industrial company you would probably want to use your company name or main brand, such as **www.gbpumpinggroup.co.uk**, or **www.gearpumps.co.uk**.
- Remember that there are no spaces in a domain name. A recent article in the *Sunday Times* mentioned that a company called Choose Spain that offers holiday villas on its website took the domain name **www.choosespain.com** and only realized its mistake when it was too late!

In the UK domain names are held with Nominet (**www.nominet.org.uk**), but registration is made via an agent, who would normally be your web hosting company.

Web hosting

A web hosting service is a type of internet hosting service that allows individuals and companies to make their own websites accessible via the world wide web. Web hosts are companies that provide space on a server they own or lease for use by their clients as well as providing internet connectivity, typically in a data centre. Web hosts can also provide data centre space and connectivity to the internet for servers they do not own to be located in their data centre.

In the early days of the web, most companies that had websites used their own equipment. They purchased their own server and employed a trained staff member to run it and to make sure that every-thing was running properly at all times. But in recent years many companies, large and small, have turned to web hosting companies instead. The site hosting companies have large banks of computers that will store all of your information for a monthly fee. Also, they are able to handle large amounts of traffic, which significantly reduces the possibility of your website crashing. For any website, the biggest potential threats include viral attacks on your system, crashes due to an extreme number of people accessing the site at the same time and theft from hackers. This is another reason why more and more companies are turning to site hosting companies. The companies offer greater security for your information as well as better protection from crashes, and at the same time you can save money on equipment and staff.

The amount of space and monthly traffic included in the hosting packages may vary, but most providers now offer a premium package with an unlimited amount of web hosting space, unlimited monthly traffic and unlimited amounts of e-mail. Most allow multiple websites and also include a number of free domain names. It is important also for you to get a dedicated IP address. (This gives you a specific server address.)

The most common types of web hosting plans include:

- *Shared hosting plan*: several websites are hosted on the same server, sharing the server's resources and using the same IP address.
- *Virtual dedicated server plan*: the server is split into multiple virtual servers, each with its own IP address.
- *Dedicated server plan*: each dedicated server customer gets their own physical server.

The UK web hosting industry is well established and competitive. There are a wide range of established companies offering packages for home web hosting, business web hosting and e-commerce web hosting. I use UK2.net, whose main competitors are currently WebFusion, 1 & 1 and Fasthosts. The best way to decide which web hosting company is best for you is to go to Hosting-Review (**www.hosting-review.com**) and click on 'UK reviews' to look at their comparison of the current 10 top UK hosting companies. The reviews include details of the companies, together with information on the range of services that each can provide and the current pricing. (Most packages are paid for on a monthly basis.)

The hosting companies also offer a 'set-up' service for those who don't have either the time or the technical expertise to set up the site themselves.

Designing and building a website

Your website is a shop window that is open 24 hours a day, seven days a week, in fact 365 days a year. So it important that your customers enjoy using your website and find it easy to navigate around.

Some important points to bear in mind when designing a website are:

- Keep it simple.
- Plan out the pages.
- Make sure that the content is relevant.
- Use pictures and images to add interest.
- Make sure that you give each page a unique web page title and web page name, and include keywords (also known as meta tags, these are a tool used by search engines to help them to determine how to rank sites in their search results).
- Make it easy for people to contact you.
- Submit your site to all the major search engines.

It is also important once your website is up and running that you regularly update the content.

Most of the web hosting companies include a site building tool such as RV Sitebuilder to help you to build your website. Although this can be quite daunting, they normally include a 'step by step' guide to help you. Before you start you need to have all of the images and content ready to go. UK2.net includes a seven-step guide to building your website:

- Create site (you have the option to create a normal website or a blog).
- Select template. (Hundreds of different templates are available under categories such as: computer and technology, travel and leisure, business, industrial, hotels and leisure.)
- Modify style.
- Select page structure.
- Design site using the WYSIWYG (what you see is what you get) design interface or edit the html code directly.
- Customize the web page titles and page names.
- Publish.

Personally I think that unless you are sure that you have the technical expertise to do this, you are much better using a web design company to design and build the website for you. Web design companies use a website designer to create the front end of your website and a web developer to work on the site's functionality and coding. Together they determine how the site is arranged and how it comes across to web users. If you decide what you want from your site and provide them with the content, the designer will work together with the developer to realize what you have in mind. There are a huge number of web design companies who design and build business websites from as little as £700. They have the knowledge to design and build a well-structured and attractive site. (Remember that customers are impatient and will not persevere around a website that is difficult to navigate.)

To select a website designer, I suggest looking on a website such as Approved Index (**www.approvedindex.co.uk**). In their section on web design services they include a wide range of web design companies. You can view all of the companies or you can narrow your search to 'Companies by area', 'Companies by city' or 'Companies by town'. So you can select a local web design company if you prefer, or look for a specialist company that specializes in particular types of websites or particular industries. They have a simple enquiry form that you can fill in to get free, no-obligation quotes from up to four web design companies. Obviously you get what you pay for and although simple websites may start at £700, you can pay many thousands of pounds for a more sophisticated design. But web designers don't just design a site to look pretty. They have a thorough understanding of how web users think and behave, and will create a design that is based on ease of usability and is designed to help maximize your profits.

Internal websites (Intranets)

Most companies have a large amount of information stored in their internal computer system that needs to be accessed and used by both internal and external staff. Much of this information may be sensitive, so it needs to be kept safe and secure, but at the same time it may need to be accessed by employees who are travelling or working from home as well as by office-based employees. Using just the internet to do this is dangerous, because it would be too easy for outsiders to gain access to sensitive information. That is why many companies have a company intranet. An intranet is a safe and secure system that is exclusive to those who work for the company. It is more secure than the internet because it has security measures that include a firewall to keep out those who are not permitted access.

If you want to set up a company intranet you need to hire a professional to do it. They can set up the system in a way that protects your information, but at the same time allows your employees access to the information, wherever they may be.

Setting up an online shop

As with an ordinary website, the options with an e-commerce site are to buy a package from a web hosting company or to have one built for you by a web design company.

The most common design is the 'shopping cart' design, where items purchased are put into a shopping cart that appears on each page as you move through the site and the goods are then paid for at the 'checkout'.

Your site needs to be easy to administer as well as easy to use and the 'shopping cart' should include the following features:

- *Administration*: you need easy-to-use administration options, including online administration and an editor on the actual page you are looking at (when logged in as the administrator). You need to be able to add unlimited numbers of products, pages and online help guides. You also need a good report function.
- *Payment*: most shopping carts come with a wide range of payment options that your administrator can enable or disable. These include credit/debit cards (online and/or over the phone), PayPal, WorldPay, SECpay, electronic funds transfer (EFT) and cash on delivery.

- *Postage and packing*: a number of options ranging from postage by weight and postage by item to orders above a certain value having free postage. It also needs to include the option of notifying customers when the goods are shipped, and of creating tracking numbers.
- *VAT and tax*: your cart needs to be able to handle different currencies and tax.
- *Security*: you need to be confident that your e-commerce hosting company has tested the cart against security threats, including the very latest problems. If you have a separate IP address, you can get your hosting company to provide you with an SSL certificate. (SSL, or Secure Socket Layer, is the global standard security technology that creates an encrypted link between a web server and a web browser to ensure that all data transmitted remain private and secure – you will recognize this as the 'golden padlock' that appears in your browser to indicate that you are viewing a secure web page.)
- *Marketing*: it should include marketing tools such as volume discounts, site promotions and e-mail campaigns.
- *Search engine optimization* (SEOs): search engine rankings are very important for any online shop and good rankings mean success. The cart should be written in SEO friendly PHP (hyper text preprocessor) and include other tools for optimizing individual products, departments and pages.
- *Product pages*: these should include tools such as customer reviews and wish lists.

Other useful website tools

Web analytics

Web analytics software allows companies to track which pages of their website are most popular, which promotions are clicked on most – basically which parts and which products seem to attract users and which parts don't. Stats 2.0 is one of the most popular web analytics tools. It allows you to monitor traffic to your website in real time.

You can track where users enter and where they leave, where they come from (which search engines, etc) and where they go next, how long they stay on the site and how many pages they look at while they are there. You can log the number of daily visitors and even where in the world they are all located. If you are getting an e-commerce package, make sure that it includes web analytics software.

RSS (really simple syndication)

An RSS feed is a code that is embedded in a web page to allow search engines to identify new content that has been added to the page. When new content is added, the RSS software advises specialist services that new content has been added, and this is then received by users who have an RSS reader installed on their computer. Some of the reader programmes are free and some are commercial. (If you use Opera or IE 7.0 Maxthon, you don't need any special software, because Opera can download and read RSS feeds.) You can get details of how to read RSS on the RSS website (**www.rss-specification.com**). (Note: at the time of writing, RSS is not officially supported by Windows, but according to the RSS website this is planned, and once it happens RSS will become the de facto standard for distributing information.)

RSS feeds are commonly provided on blogs and also on newspaper, magazine and television websites. But it is becoming common for most major websites to provide RSS feeds. All major hi-tech companies, such as Microsoft, Google, IBM and Apple, already distribute their press releases using RSS. Many companies now use it to distribute information about price list updates and new product information as well as various company news items. It also has many applications in advertising and sales promotions.

Social media

Social networking

Social networking sites are micro-websites that allow people to set up a personal profile and then interact to share information with a range of other users (usually those accepted as 'friends'). It is easy to add photos, music and videos.

There are a huge number of social networking sites appealing to different types of social groups. Some have grown in popularity, but many have fallen by the wayside. By far the most popular sites are:

- *Facebook*: with over 500 million users, Facebook is the largest of the social networking sites. From its early beginnings as a site for students, Facebook has rapidly become *the* social networking site. Although it is just that – a social networking site – there are growing opportunities for companies, either in setting up their own dedicated Facebook site or Facebook 'group', or in creating a Facebook application or advert.
- *MySpace*: second to Facebook, with about 300 million registered users. It is still a major player, but its audience has been declining since the rise of Facebook in 2008. Figures issued in July 2010 by ComScore, a market research company, showed that UK visitors to MySpace halved from 6.5 million to just 3.3 million between May 2009 and May 2010.
- *Bebo*: Bebo is a popular site with teenagers and the under 30s. It was put up for sale by AOL and sold to a small venture capital company in 2010 after worldwide user figures had dropped from a peak of 40 million to just 12 million as of February 2010.
- *Twitter*: a microblogging site with 124 million registered users. As of May 2010 its user base in the UK was 4.3 million (up 62 per cent from the previous year). Its microblogging system only allows messages of 140 characters; some believe that this makes it more acceptable for business as the messages are less invasive than e-mails.
- *LinkedIn*: this is a business-to-business site that allows business people to find each another, stay in touch, find out about new jobs or business opportunities and network to share advice and information. It has about 10 million users.
- *Xing*: Xing advertises itself as 'Global networking for professionals'. It has similar aims to LinkedIn and claims to have over 9 million members in 200 countries.

Much more information on how to use social networking sites to promote your business is included in Chapters 5 and 7.

Blogs

A blog (short for 'web log') is a type of website or part of a website. Blogs started as personal websites written by individuals who were passionate about a topic and wanted to share it with the rest of the online community. Blogs are usually maintained by an individual with regular entries of commentary, descriptions of events or other material such as graphics or video. Entries are commonly displayed in reverse-chronological order. Most blogs allow readers to add their own comments. Blogs are usually edited online through a web browser, so this means that they can be created or added to by people with virtually no knowledge of web technology. Because blogs are web pages, it is possible to embed pictures, video and audio files. As of December 2007, the blog search engine Technorati was tracking more than 112 million blogs. Because they are web pages, many people do not differentiate them from other web pages when they see them.

Although it was initially a social networking tool, blogging is increasingly being used by businesses. Many companies find that setting up a blog on their own website and encouraging customers to use it is a useful way of getting feedback and keeping in touch with their customers. Some companies also have internal blogs (which are not accessible to the general public) and encourage their staff to read the material on the blog and write or add content to it.

Microblogs

Microblogging is a type of blogging where there is only a very limited amount of space available for text. (Usually a maximum of 140 characters). The most popular microblogging service is Twitter (**www. twitter.com**). At the time of writing there were a number of competing services offered by companies such as FriendFeed and Jaiku. Popular social networking sites such as Facebook and MySpace also have an embedded microblogging feature, such as the 'status update' feature on Facebook. Each entry that is made on Twitter is called a 'tweet' and some people call using Twitter 'tweeting'. The advantage of micro-blogs is that they can be accessed by mobile phone as well as by PC/laptop. This allows instant feedback on an event. An example could be someone having a good (or bad!) experience at a top London restaurant 'tweeting' their approval or disapproval before they have even left the restaurant. This clearly has implications for companies, because now feedback on their products can be instantaneous.

Video and photo sharing

The most popular video sharing site is YouTube (**www.youtube.com**). It allows people to upload, watch and share videos. YouTube has over 300 million users worldwide and like Facebook it has opportunities for companies to upload their own video and to advertise on the site.

Flickr (**www.flickr.com**) is the most popular site for sharing and commenting on photos. Even Buckingham Palace has YouTube and Flickr sites!

Wikis

A wiki is a form of website that anybody can edit and update. Wikis are mostly used within companies to allow groups of people to create and edit material to form an evolving body of knowledge for the group. The most popular online wiki is Wikipedia (**www.wikipedia.com**). Wikipedia is a free online encyclopaedia and is now one of the largest reference websites in existence.

What does the future hold?

If I really knew what the future holds then I would be a rich man, but I think that we can already see some clear signs.

Hardware platforms are converging, internet and mobile phone technologies are converging and this convergence will continue. Only 10 years ago a mobile phone was a mobile phone and a laptop computer or PC was just a computer. Admittedly even then there was some connectivity. Even back in 1999 I was able to connect my Nokia mobile phone to my laptop to send and receive e-mails if I could find a good signal, but that was the limit of what was possible. Convergence has been gradually creeping up on us – text messaging on mobiles, Blackberries to send e-mails on the move, internet access via mobile phones. Adding camera and video functions to mobile phones made it only a matter of time before devices became available that would allow people to watch TV on their phones. Netbooks were added to the range of available devices, so that you didn't need to carry your laptop with you, just to stay in touch.

To most people the clear difference between mobile phones on the one hand and laptops and PCs on the other was size – not just the physical size of the device, but the size of the screen and the size and flexibility of the keypad. But then came the voice-to-text app. When the iPhone was launched in 2007 there were no apps (mobile phone applications) written for it, but when the iPad was launched in the UK in May 2010 there were already 6,500 apps available for it. These include the Dragon Dictation app, which is available for use on the iPhone and also on other types of smartphone. It allows users to speak a message of any length into the phone, press a button and wait while the sounds are recreated as written words on the screen. Users can then decide if they want to send the message as a text message or as an e-mail.

At the time of writing, Apple's app store could offer more than 225,000 apps and there were more than 100,000 apps available for Google's Android. According to Jupiter research, global app downloads will rise from 2.6 billion in 2009 to more than 25 billion in 2015. The *Annual Communications Market Report* from Ofcom for 2010 reported that the number of people in the UK using their mobile phones to surf the web had risen from 5.7 million in 2008 to 13.5 million by August 2010.

A few years ago, it was considered an innovation when airlines set up a facility for passengers to check in and choose their seat online and then print off their own boarding card at home or in the office. But now you have the 'mobile boarding pass'. Passengers on some airlines, including British Airways, can download an app that allows them not only to check in using their phone, but also to press a button on the app, which then displays their boarding pass containing a bar code on the screen. This can be used just like a normal boarding pass and be scanned at the departure gate.

So now there is technically no real difference between a text message and an e-mail and we are gradually finding that most of what can be carried out on a PC/laptop can also be accomplished using other devices if you are on the move.

Summary

- The internet is just about the most important tool available to help you to grow your business. A quarter of the world's population now use it.
- It provides a major sales channel for all types of products and most companies of any size now have online purchasing.
- Most industrial companies also use their websites to provide information on their products and to publicize new products and sales successes.
- Your domain name is the title and address of your website. Most companies try to buy a domain name that says something about their business or incorporates their main brand or company name.
- Web hosts are companies that provide space on a server for use by their clients as well as providing internet connectivity. More and more companies are using them, because they offer greater security for your information as well as better protection from crashes, and at the same time they can save you money on equipment and staff.
- Your website is a shop window that is open 24 hours a day seven days a week. It is important that your customers enjoy using your website and find it easy to navigate around.
- A company intranet is a safe and secure internal system, protected by a firewall. It is exclusive to those who work for a company.
- Depending of its complexity, you can buy an e-commerce package from a web hosting company or have one built for you by a web design company. The most common design of online shop uses the 'shopping cart' design.

- Web analytics software allows companies to monitor traffic to their websites in real time.
- Social networking sites are micro-websites that allow people to set up a personal profile and then to interact to share information with other users. From a business point of view the most important sites are Facebook, LinkedIn and Twitter (which is a microblogging service). Blogs, microblogs and video and photo sharing sites such as YouTube and Flickr all have business uses.
- Hardware platforms are converging, internet and mobile phone technologies are converging and this convergence will continue.

Chapter five
The role of public relations in the internet age

There are a wide variety of definitions of PR, each emphasizing a slightly different approach and each trying to give a brief and concise definition of a complex and diverse subject.

The Chartered Institute of Public Relations is the largest public relations organization in Europe, with over 9,500 members involved in all aspects of communications. On its website (**www.cipr.co.uk**) it defines public relations as follows:

> Public relations is about reputation – the result of what you do, what you say and what others say about you. Public relations is the discipline which looks after reputation, with the aim of earning understanding and support and influencing opinion and behaviour. It is the planned and sustained effort to establish and maintain goodwill and mutual understanding between an organisation and its publics.

A few years ago the PR guru Frank Jefkins expanded on the key concepts in the definition:

- *Deliberate, planned and sustained*: organized as a campaign or programme and therefore not haphazard. A continuous effort.
- *Establish and maintain*: create and retain the goodwill. Important concept as this is the main objective of PR.
- *Mutual understanding*: make an organization understood to others. By being understood, it is hoped that goodwill is built up.

Public relations is all about communication – both internal and external. Communication is playing an increasingly important role today, not only in everyday life, but also in the business world. Communication and public relations are closely linked to each other. Public relations is an important part of marketing and, apart from its main objective of creating and maintaining goodwill for an organization, it is used to great effect to enhance advertising, sales promotion – even exhibitions and conferences. No business can be successful without the effective use of public relations.

Public relations has sometimes had a bad press in recent years. Some people associate it with propaganda, publicity and whitewashing, and certainly the use of spin doctors in politics has encouraged this view. Also it seems that whenever there is a scandal or exposé in public life, it is reported that the person concerned has taken on the services of a 'public relations expert'. This is part of the crisis management side of PR, which has grown in the last decade. Crisis management helps organizations and individuals to cope with a situation of any kind and to come out of it with some form of credibility. It was noticeable that when oil spilled into the Gulf of Mexico in May 2010, BP initiated a major response effort to contain the oil and at the same time instructed a PR firm to help contain the damage to its reputation. Unfortunately for BP's crisis management team, their CEO made two huge errors that are a no-no in crisis management. He underestimated the problem – 'The impact will be very small' – and he managed to sound selfish and flippant – 'I want my life back'. This is perhaps what some people see as the negative side of public relations. But at the other end of the spectrum public relations is also used to promote sporting and charitable events. So it is clear that different people have different ideas of what public relations is and what it can or should be able to achieve. Public relations is central to business communication. It is a powerful industry that is growing and steadily gaining respect as it does so.

Nowadays, it is not just governments and large corporations that have their own PR departments. All organizations of any size see the need to take on a communications professional. It is generally accepted that communication, using public relations, is vital to many aspects of business – in both the private and the public sector. There has been a large increase in the use of public relations over the last 10 years or so, and now even universities and large local councils will have their own public relations and press office.

Small companies also need to use public relations, but they will often not even have a separate marketing department and certainly not be able to justify employing a public relations professional. In small companies the same person who does the marketing (probably the managing director or sales director) will probably also handle the public relations. That does not necessarily mean that they will do all the work themselves. They will probably use the services of a public relations consultancy or a marketing agency/consultancy that also handles public relations work.

Public relations is an important and adaptable marketing communications tool. But communication is not just one way. It is a two-way process and the information that you get back can be just as important as the information that you send out. This is reactive and proactive PR.

You may think that public relations is just an external marketing tool that you would use to communicate with the outside world. But it can be employed both inside and outside your organization. Internally, public relations can be used to effectively develop a unified internal organizational culture. It can help a company to develop a team spirit, with everyone understanding the mutual marketing goals that they are working towards. In this respect the human resources and public relations departments would work hand in hand.

In this chapter we are primarily concerned with external communication. External communication is with a company's external 'publics'. ('Publics' is PR-speak for the range of different target audiences that a company would be aiming its public relations at. This includes existing and potential customers, investors, the media, suppliers and opinion formers.) External communication can cover anything and everything relating to the company itself, but particularly its image and its brand images. From a marketing point of view it also includes the communication of information relating to the company's products, promotions and channels to market.

The PR resource

In large organizations the main public relations resource will usually be either a full public relations department or a single public relations professional. In small companies there may well be no separate in-house public relations resource. But even in a large organization there will normally be some type of external resource. Public relations departments will not usually attempt to carry out all public relations work themselves, because they will not be experts in all aspects of public relations. Even large companies often use a public relations consultancy for major individual projects in areas such as image, branding and sponsorship. Specialist services such as in-house magazine production and conference organization and management are frequently farmed out.

In the UK there are a wide range of public relations consultancies. Although there are a number of major international consultancies, there are also many medium and smaller companies and even individual consultants. Many of these are members of the Public Relations Consultants Association (PRCA – **www.prca.org.uk**). The advantage to a small company of using an external resource is that you only pay for the time that you use. So you can use the consultancy for 'one-off' assignments, to supply specialist services such as a media-relations service, or to plan and execute a complete public relations programme.

One disadvantage for a large company is that the consultancy may not initially be familiar with the company culture. You are also charged strictly by the hour or day, which means that overtime and going the extra mile, which can easily be done in-house, cost extra when using a consultancy. The agency's personnel are loyal first to their agency and then to the clients. They are also obliged to maintain a good relationship with the media, so there are more potential conflicts of interest. These are reasons why many larger companies only use consultants for specific projects.

The public relations programme – objectives and strategies

All public relations activities should have planned objectives. You need to decide whom you want to influence and what you want to say to them. Then you need to prepare the programme. The programme is the 'strategy' and the individual activities are the 'tactics'. In planning a public relations programme you should take the following steps:

1 Appraise the situation.
2 Set your objectives.
3 Define your target audience(s).
4 Select the media and techniques to be used.
5 Prepare your budget.
6 Assess the results (once the activity has been carried out).

To be successful, public relations activities should last for a reasonable period of time. Even if they are focused on an individual project such as a product launch, the public relations activities should start several months before the planned launch and continue for several months afterwards. Ideally any public relations programme should be designed to last for at least 12 months.

Some tools used in public relations

Press releases

A traditional tool of the trade is the press release. This is a newsworthy press story that has been put together, usually with a photograph included. It could be about a new product, a key appointment in your company, a major contract you have received, an expansion of your factory – in fact anything that you think could get you some press coverage. But remember that it must be newsworthy. A press release is not an advertisement, and if it looks like one it will not be used.

In the days of the printed word, when everything was sent by post, it was normal to keep a press release to one page. Nowadays, press releases are sent by e-mail (or by using RSS) but the same rule applies. Some companies screen e-mails with attachments and block them, so it is common for press releases to be sent with the text and photograph pasted into the e-mail. If a paper or magazine decides to use your press release they will then request a higher resolution version of the photograph. You should send them a photograph with a resolution of at least 300 dpi.

Remember that editors are busy people. An eye-catching strapline in the e-mail subject heading is a plus, as many e-mails are not even opened.

But certainly make sure that your key message is in the first sentence. If you don't attract the editor's attention immediately, they will probably not go past the first paragraph and your press release will end up in the recycle bin.

The type of content should also be varied depending on the section of the press you are sending your press release to. The trade press will expect more technical detail than your local paper.

A press release is a specific news item sent to a target audience. Most importantly, a press release needs to have a news hook – a clear piece of news that will be of interest to the media. It is not a general e-mailshot. The target audience is made up mainly of newspapers and magazines, but will often also include television companies and radio stations. Your company's circulation list will be specific to you and should be separated into different categories. A typical list of categories could be:

- trade press;
- national press;
- local press;
- local/regional TV and radio.

For each entity on the list you should have a contact name, e-mail address, telephone number and the company address. Since people move jobs, you should check the contact names and their contact details regularly – there is no point in sending your press release to someone who is no longer there!

Feature articles

A feature article is another way of getting coverage for your company and its products. It is normally written exclusively for one publication and may not be reproduced elsewhere or put into any other publication without the permission of the magazine that it was written for. Having said that, once you have the text, clearly you can reuse or rewrite parts of it for other uses. It is not just a long news item and must contain material that will be of significant interest to the magazine's wider readership. It is not an 'advertorial' and should be seen as a serious article. For example a specialist pump manufacturer might approach a magazine like *Fluid Handling* and ask if they were interested in a feature article on pumping concrete. The company knows that it has particular expertise in this field and can write the article in such a way that it is made clear that they are the world leader in this field. Similarly, a director of a travel company may write a comment piece for a trade magazine on current trends in travel or on legislation affecting the industry. Becoming a recognized spokesperson for the industry is useful because a journalist may then come to this person for a quotation and the company name will be mentioned: eg 'Noel Smith, managing director of Sunway Holidays, said: ...'.

In agreeing to the feature article the magazine would probably try to persuade the company to take advertising space in the edition of the magazine in which the article is published. It may even be prepared to offer the company a price for a specific number of reprints of the article. So the company gets something that can be used like a brochure or data sheet as well.

A further advantage of a feature article is that the magazines containing the articles are frequently kept in libraries and can be used as reference material for a significant period of time.

Press kits

Press kits (sometimes called press packs) are used at exhibitions. Most major exhibitions will have a press office where press kits can be collected by the press. A press kit should include a selection of relevant and newsworthy press releases, together with brochures, photos and other background material on your company and the products that you are exhibiting. But don't forget that at a major exhibition there will be hundreds and in some cases (such as the Achema in Frankfurt, Germany) thousands of stands. So the press will be selective. They will only take what they feel they can use and may not take your kit if it is too bulky and contains lots of non-news items.

Key channels of communication used in public relations

Television

Television has coped rather well with technological change. Whereas newspapers are dying, television has been fighting back by expanding into cable and satellite. Where once television viewers were restricted to a handful of TV channels, now most can access hundreds. India, for example, has gone from two channels in the 1990s to over 600 in 2010. Many TV companies are now building online-subscription video services and other services that they hope will help them to compete in the internet world.

Because airtime on television is very expensive, most 'image' or 'PR' advertising is carried out by major corporations and multinationals. Having said that, television has huge audiences and if you can get your message onto television, it can have a greater impact than through any other medium.

You can really forget about getting news coverage on national television unless you are launching something like the iPad or planning to invest in a new factory with the creation of thousands of jobs. Local or regional television is more open to 'interesting' local company news items such as new products, large export orders or factory expansion plans. The BBC has regional news programmes like *South East Today*, and also regional current affairs programmes like *Inside Out*. Regional television programmes will display their website details, e-mail address and a phone number at the end of each broadcast. Before contacting them, you should do your homework. Look on their website and also phone them to get a contact name to e-mail your material to. E-mail your press release and follow up with another phone call.

Remember that news programmes are only interested in current news – so if they are interested they will probably want you to come into their studio or send someone to interview you at short notice. Even if it takes a few days for them to respond, they will then probably want to see you on the same day or the next. Television is visual, so take some product or photographs with you, or if the interview takes place in your company make sure that there is product in the shot. Remember that most television is not live and even short pieces for 'live' news programmes will be edited down to fit the slot time allocated. So just because you are interviewed on camera for 10 minutes, don't be surprised if the 'on screen' time is only one or two minutes at most. It is therefore important to have a note of the few 'key points' that you want to get over and to make sure that you discuss these with the interviewer prior to the recorded interview.

Radio

Buying airtime on radio is much less expensive than buying airtime on television and there are a wide range of local and regional commercial radio stations as well as nationwide stations like Classic FM. Local radio can be a good channel for small local businesses to use. Unlike television, radio is not restricted to indoor audiences. It can be listened to in the car or on a portable device like a combined MP3 player/radio virtually anywhere. It is important to remember that most people listen to the radio while doing other things, so any radio 'image' advertising that you do will rely on repetition to have any effect. Repetition is also important, because there is no visual side to radio and the human brain reacts less strongly to audio stimulation than it does to images.

National press

The national press is mainly interested in national and international news that will interest their readers around the whole country. They are not interested in news that will only have local or regional interest. This means that only large or multinational companies are likely to be able to use national newspapers for their public relations. In fact in most cases the only way that they get coverage is by buying advertising space and using it for image advertising. Typical types of companies that do this are major banks, energy companies, airlines, car manufacturers, etc.

Local press

The local press is of much more importance to small and medium-sized companies because the readers are interested in local news. A factory expansion, important foreign customers visiting the town, your new sales manager – these are all things that would interest your local paper. But they are also trying to survive by selling advertising, so you may find that you get the best coverage when you provide 'advertorial' – a mixture of a news story and an advert in a special business section.

Trade press

Although many companies are only interested in the national media, the trade press is by far the most important PR outlet for industrial companies. Because the readers will understand the applications and products you can include much more technical content in your press releases.

The internet

Traditionally television, radio, the national and local press and the trade press have been used for both public relations and advertising. Although these are all still used to a greater or lesser degree, the development of the internet has added an additional very powerful communication channel. In fact the internet is rapidly becoming the vehicle of choice for public relations. Most companies now publish their press releases as news items on their website. These items will be viewed by customers, competitors and other interested parties, and some of these people may also transmit them further via blogs or other means. The rise of the internet and social media has given PR a big boost. Not only has much public relations work and advertising been transferred to the internet but the older media have also been transferring themselves in part to the internet. The BBC iPlayer now accounts for a significant amount of UK internet traffic with 123 million television and radio programmes being viewed in April 2010 alone! There is also a convergence between hardware platforms such as computers and mobile phones, with both now able to access the internet and download whatever the bandwidth will take and the user can afford to pay for.

External media support

To get the best out of the media, you need to have contacts and know how to get your message across to them. For this reason many companies that would manage their own PR for other areas, choose to use a public relations consultancy to handle their media relations. The consultancy may use specific contacts and their own circulation lists for sending out press releases, but they may also use a major news agency such as the Press Association or Reuters to help them for specific campaigns. Major news agencies have press release and photo distribution services that allow them to send text and images directly into the newsrooms of the media in the UK and beyond.

Advertising vs PR?

According to data from Veronis Suhler Stevenson, a private equity company, spending on public relations in the United States grew by more than 4 per cent in 2008 and 3 per cent in 2009 whereas spending on advertising contracted by nearly 3 per cent in 2008 and 8 per cent in 2009. Spending on word-of-mouth marketing, including managing services such as outreach to bloggers, increased by more than 10 per cent in 2009. One of the reasons that PR has done so well is that a PR campaign is often cheaper than mass advertising and its impact, in terms of coverage in the media or online, can be measured more easily. Taking a full-page colour advertisement in the main section of the *Sunday Times* will cost a multinational company nearly £100,000. Getting the company mentioned in an article could cost a few thousand pounds or even less in a small, targeted PR campaign. This is why so many companies cut the advertising budget but retain PR – it's much cheaper and much more trusted. The trust issue is also key. People trust the news media so an article mentioning the benefits of a product is trusted far more than an advertisement, often at a fraction of the cost too.

Online public relations

There is a lot of hype about online public relations and the changing relationship between public relations, advertising and other aspects of marketing. There is no doubt that the goalposts have changed, and there is also no doubt that they will continue to change even more rapidly in the future. In 2003 Tim O'Reilly of O'Reilly Media used the designation 'web 2.0' to cover the evolution of the web from being a receptacle for information and communication technologies to becoming a place where people can transfer both knowledge and conversation. In its simplest terms, the 'traditional' transfer of information on the web was 'vertical'. You accessed a piece of information on the internet and downloaded the information onto your PC, laptop or mobile phone. You accessed a website and purchased an item online. The website responded with an e-mailed order confirmation and delivery advice. What is now available on the internet (web 2.0) is the 'horizontal' or 'symmetrical' transfer of information – in all directions. This 'information' can be text, conversation, images, video, in fact any means of electronic communication that is currently available. 'Information' is transferred using channels such as social networking sites (Facebook, MySpace, LinkedIn) and the rapidly developing use of, amongst others, instant messaging, blogs and particularly microblogs like Twitter. This has immense implications for all of us, but particularly for public relations. It means that any information put onto the web can be transferred and modified again and again.

Sending press releases out online

In addition to sending your press release out yourself, there are a range of online companies that specialize in distributing press releases to major news sites and search engines on the web. Some sites, such as PR.com (**www.pr.com**), will post your press release for free, but obviously most charge for the service. There are many such companies available, but some of the better known are PRWeb (**www.prweb.com** – **www.uk.prweb.com** in the UK), PR Newswire (**www.prnewswire.com** – **www.prnewswire.co.uk** in the UK) and Business Wire (**www.businesswire.com**).

Developing your social media strategy

Using social media as a PR channel for your company is a fairly straightforward concept. The beauty is that it is just as easy (if not easier) for a small company as for a large multinational corporation. A small company is likely to react to comments on its user blog and answer messages on its Facebook account more quickly than a large corporation might do and this is important. To get started, the types of things you need to do are to set up your own blog on your website, create a presence on Facebook and create a Twitter account. Sounds easy, doesn't it? No, its not as easy as it sounds. Earlier in this chapter we said that all public relations activities should have planned objectives – you need to decide whom you want to influence and you need to prepare a programme.

When you decide that you want to take your PR online, I would recommend the following:

- Take advice from a consultancy to help you develop a social media strategy. Bear in mind that you may need to develop several strategies, each tailored to a different social media channel.
- Make sure that you have an adequate and ongoing dedicated resource to manage your social media programme. (This may need to be a dedicated person.) Once you have set up the sites, you need to continue to put material on them regularly and to respond to any criticisms within 24 hours.

Once you are up and running, remember that to be successful you need to interact properly with your customers. Don't put information on your blog just because it interests you. Listen to what people have to say. Don't ignore criticism – respond, and respond quickly. This is another thing that PR consultants can help you with. They can track what your customers are saying about you online and respond directly to any negative commentary that is building up. Because social media is not just a two-way conversation, you will see that certain points raised on your blog or Facebook group by one person will be commented on or responded to by others.

Netiquette

In a recent article for *Springboard*, the UK Trade & Investment magazine, the independent PR consultant Dinah Hatch listed the social conventions for companies using social networks. I've also added one or two of my own.

The dos

- *Listen.* This is your opportunity to find out what your customers really think and remedy any issues they may have with your products or services.
- *Make time.* It is not a quick process. Track and measure the success of what you are doing.
- *Be responsive.* Respond within 24 hours.
- *Let go of your content.* Be aware that people will take your company video, re-edit it, and take the mickey out of you. You are operating in a different world. But in the end your blog will be self-regulated by your brand's devotees.
- *Take care with how you express yourself.* The web is infamous for satire and very easy for building high levels of feedback. Negative comments can snowball. If you make a mistake, you may be ripped to pieces by web users. Note that defamation and offensive language are far more difficult to police on the web.
- *Know your culture and be aware that it changes.* Understand that moderating a blog about your brand does not mean not allowing

anything other than the company line to be said. If you do, and a blog is too antiseptic, people will smell a rat.

- Remember that the barrier to entry may be low, but the standards expected of your presence online are high, so you must plan your campaign.

The don'ts

- *Never contravene the mores of a site.* One car hire company delayed for seven days before responding to a criticism of their brand in a blog and then replied via a lawyer's letter. The firm was roundly derided by the online community for its heavy-handed approach.
- Don't hijack other subject matter to get noticed or treat social networks as direct sales tools.
- *Don't ignore bad comments,* engage with them as well.

How does it work in practice?

In July 2010 Gatwick Airport launched a Twitter feed (@gatwick_airport) to publish updates about the airport and to encourage direct feedback. Most airports and airlines are now attempting to use some form of direct Twitter communication. Twitter can be a much more effective way of making a complaint, than phoning a customer service number. Experience shows that companies respond much more quickly and efficiently when people tweet their complaints.

On their website UK Trade & Investment (**www.ukti.gov.uk**) have integrated social media feeds to the UKTI blog (with RSS to send you updates by e-mail), Twitter (if you join they will send you short, timely messages), Flickr (showing the UKTI photostream), YouTube (the UKTIWeb's channel with videos) and LinkedIn (you can join the UKTI group). In a recent edition of the magazine *Springboard*, Kate Sbuttoni, online communications manager at UKTI, said:

> We put out about 10 tweets daily about what UK Trade & Investment is doing, alongside content on our LinkedIn group. We have found these are really useful tools for driving attendance to our events and raising awareness generally about how we can help business. We include links

to our website and have found that LinkedIn and Twitter are in the top five sites that refer traffic to our site. But we don't just use social media sites for pushing a message out. It's also about engaging with and understanding our market.

As you can see from the above examples, you can get a lot out of using social media if you are prepared to make the investment and then work at it. But it is not something that you can start off and then expect to run by itself.

Online public relations is a complex and continually evolving subject. For really comprehensive and up-to-date expert coverage I would suggest you read: *Online Public Relations: A practical guide to developing an online strategy in the world of social media* by David Phillips and Philip Young. This book is part of the 'PR In Practice Series' published by Kogan Page. Or for the US, view: *The New Rules of Marketing & PR* by David Meerman Scott.

Other roles of public relations

PR support for exhibitions, trade fairs, etc

The main reason for taking part in an exhibition or trade fair is to get your company and its products more widely known to a particular target audience. Although involved in many aspects of exhibitions, the key areas of public relations support are in publicizing your involvement in the exhibition, both before it starts and while it is on. This involves preparing and circulating press releases, preparing catalogue entries and exhibition website entries, and the preparation and dissemination of press kits at the exhibition itself.

The mechanics of organizing an exhibition and setting up and running your own stand are covered in detail in Chapter 8.

Conferences

A conference is a good method of communication and is used extensively in business. A conference normally covers a number of different topics with a common theme. There will often be a small trade exhibition running concurrently at the same time in the same venue (as with the political party conferences or small industry-specific conferences). It is also common to have a smaller conference running concurrently with a major exhibition – as is the case with Achema (for the chemical industry), which takes place every three years in Frankfurt, Germany, or Weftec (for water and waste treatment), which takes place annually in the United States in a different city each time.

Key areas where companies use conferences are:

- the management conference;
- the sales conference;
- the distributor conference.

The management conference

Management conferences would normally include senior and middle management and the number of delegates could be anything from 100 to 500, although 250 is probably typical. They would take place every 12–18 months and would have a number of objectives:

- to pass on clear management messages to all;
- to provide management with examples of success created with different products or in different geographical regions;
- to allow the interchange of information between the different delegates;
- team building;
- to send everyone away recharged.

The sales conference

The sales conference is not just a normal sales meeting that would take place in one area or one country on a regular basis. It is a conference involving sales and marketing personnel from different separate entities within the company or group. It could be a national conference or, for a multinational company, it could include personnel from all areas of the world where the company is active. It would be a much smaller gathering than a management conference and could involve as few as 20 or as many as 100 delegates. It has much the same aims as the management conference, but with the emphasis on sales and growing them.

The distributor conference

The distributor conference is similar to the sales conference, but involves a company's outside distribution. The delegates would normally be the key sales and management personnel from a company's major distributors. Again, the number of delegates would probably be between 20 and 100.

Company conferences are normally organized to take place in the early autumn – September to early November, so that they can impact on the budgeting process for the following year. It is typical for such a conference to last between two and four days. Since delegates will have come in from different places, often different countries or even continents, these conferences are always residential.

I would make the following suggestion. If your conference is small – say up to about 30 delegates – you can consider organizing it all yourself. If it is larger than that, then it is a false economy not to use expert help for at least some, if not all, of the conference organization. If you are not an expert you are sure to forget something, and if things go wrong the negative impact can be such that it would have been better if the conference had not taken place at all.

I was once given the job of Vice President Communications for a major multinational company on condition that I organized a senior management conference for 250 key executives set in a nice Mediterranean location 12 weeks from the date of my appointment! I would not have been able to organize this if I had tried to do everything myself. I set up my management team from my marketing department and they concentrated on sorting out the agenda, organizing the speakers, getting their basic presentations and turning them into good PowerPoint presentations. I decided to use the services of an event management company, and on the basis of peer recommendation I chose WorldEvents (**www.worldevents.com**). Once I had explained the brief to them and agreed approximate pricing, based on an approximate agenda, they were able to help me choose a venue and go from there. We selected Cyprus and they gave me a selection of five or six hotels that they knew that had facilities to handle a conference of this size. I then travelled to Cyprus with a manager of WorldEvents and visited the hotels, a number of sites for team building and a selection of restaurants for evening events. I was able to decide there and then on the hotel venue and the venues for other things. So within three weeks of starting I had everything booked and everyone invited. WorldEvents also supplied the audio visual equipment (through a local supplier), ran the team-building events and coordinated the transformation of basic presentations into a quality presentation package. Although we had invited all the delegates and received details of their travel arrangements, we used WorldEvents to arrange reception and airport transfers. The result was a highly professional, highly successful conference that people in the company were talking about for years to come.

PR support for product launches

The planning of a product launch combines many of the same activities as organizing conferences and exhibitions. You need a venue, you need product (or product samples), you need a programme and you need to get the right people there.

Even though the general public may see the launch of a high-profile product as something that happens on one day, many companies will take two days or even more. Within the two-day time frame it is common to have separate launch events for your different target audiences. These target audiences could be:

- the press;
- key customers;
- company staff;
- key distributors.

The company and distributor launches would be internal affairs and would normally take place before the press and customer launches. More information would be given out at the internal launches, including details of sales arguments and sales tools as well as an appraisal of the competition.

The press and customer launches would be more high profile events and would concentrate on the features and benefits of the product. As at an exhibition, press kits would be provided.

A typical action plan for a new product launch would include the following steps:

- preparing launch package;
- manufacturing exhibition-quality samples;
- booking venues and hotels;
- booking advertising;
- sending out invitations.

Preparing the launch package itself could include producing:

- a press release;
- a leaflet or brochure;
- a press advert;
- samples or 'giveaways'.

Everything about a product launch needs to support the quality of the product. So the venue itself is important and should be upmarket. If you are a small company, it can be a false economy to hold the launch at your factory to keep costs down. Better to use a good hotel with excellent audio-visual facilities.

Remember that, while you may be very excited about your new product, the media will not be unless you give them an interesting news hook or unique selling point to latch on to. Even if you've spent millions on this new product, if the news angle for the media isn't right, they won't bite!

An example of a product launch is given in Chapter 9.

Sponsorship

Sponsorship is a business arrangement that should be of benefit to both the sponsor and the sponsored. It involves the company that is the sponsor paying money to support an individual, an organization or an idea. It can take many forms, ranging from sponsoring a local roundabout to sponsoring a Premier League football team or test cricket series. It also includes endorsement, where the money is paid to the organization or individual in return for their agreeing to use specific items provided by the sponsor. These are typically items of clothing or sports equipment, such as running shoes for an athlete or polo shirts for a golfer. Although some companies may get involved in sponsorship for purely philanthropic reasons, most companies do it for either purely commercial reasons or a mixture of both.

The main commercial reason for getting involved in sponsorship is to be able to communicate the name of your company or its brand to a wide audience. Having said that, it can also be good PR if you are seen to be supporting an activity. This is particularly true for local sponsorship, where the goodwill that it generates can have a positive effect on the sales of a company's products or services, and can also help a company be seen as a more compassionate and caring employer.

The main forms of sponsorship are:

- *Sport*: this is the largest area of sponsorship activity. Sport sponsorship ranges from motor racing and round-the-world yacht races to the sponsorship of individual tennis stars.
- *The arts*: sponsorship here ranges from support for an individual exhibition or theatre performance to supporting a season of opera at Glyndebourne.
- *Exhibitions and events*: these are often sponsored by trade associations or commercial organizations. The Society of Motor Manufacturers and Traders supports the Motor Show and National Savings & Investments supports the Classical BRIT Awards.
- *Local sponsorship*: this can range from support for a local motor show or local sporting event to the sponsorship of a roundabout or a local youth football team, where the sponsor usually provides football kit, including shirts with the company name or logo.

Sponsorship is seen by many companies as a proactive form of PR that can also be very satisfying. But companies should be clear on why they decide to sponsor and should evaluate carefully the objectives and benefits of any proposal that they receive.

Summary

- Public relations is about reputation – the result of what you do, what you say and what others say about you. Its main objective is to create and retain goodwill.
- Public relations is an important and adaptable marketing communications tool. It is a two-way process and the information that you get back is just as important as the information that you send out.
- Even large companies often use a public relations consultancy for major projects in areas such as image, branding, sponsorship and the organization and management of conferences.
- All public relations activities should have planned objectives. You need to decide whom you want to influence and what you want to say to them. Then you need to prepare a programme.
- A press release is a newsworthy press story the purpose of which is to get press coverage for your company.
- A feature article is an extensive and informed article written exclusively for one publication. It is another way of getting coverage for a company and its products.
- Television, radio, the national and local press and the trade press are traditional channels of communications used in public relations.
- The internet has added a further very powerful communication tool that allows the 'horizontal' or 'symmetrical' transfer of information in all directions. This 'information' can be text, conversation, images or video, and is transferred via channels such as social networking sites and the rapidly developing use of instant messaging, blogs and microblogs like Twitter.
- Using social media as a PR channel for your company is a fairly straightforward concept, but you need to take advice from a consultancy to help you develop a social media strategy.
- Once you have set up the sites, you need to continue to put material on them regularly and to respond to any criticisms within 24 hours.

- Blogs and microblogs like Twitter can be a much more effective way for dissatisfied customers to make complaints than using the phone. Experience shows that companies respond much more quickly when people 'tweet' their complaints.
- PR has many other uses, including supporting exhibitions and trade fairs, organizing company conferences and product launches, and managing company sponsorship activities.

Chapter six
Channels to market

When customers buy your products, they expect to receive them in good time and in good order with no hassle. If they don't, they probably won't come back to buy from you again. The distribution of your products is therefore key to the success of your business. So before you can even think of planning your advertising and sales promotion, you need to do an audit of your distribution and make sure that you are taking full advantage of all of the best potential channels to market for your product and your business from those available. To most people, distribution means the physical distribution of goods. But this is only one aspect.

Distribution involves:

- marketing channels;
- physical distribution;
- customer service.

Marketing channels

Marketing channels are the means that a company can select to get into contact with its potential customers. If those people are unaware of the product, they will not buy it. There are a wide variety of different channels that a company can use. Figure 6.1 shows a typical selection of available marketing channels.

Direct sales is an expensive channel to operate and is mainly restricted to high-value industrial goods. Consumer goods are generally

FIGURE 6.1   Marketing channels

sold through distributors, wholesalers and retailers rather than through direct selling, but it is usually still necessary for the company to have a salesforce to sell to these distributors, wholesalers and retailers. Small businesses operating in a local environment will normally carry out direct sales, whether they are offering a service or a commodity.

The effect of 'needs' on purchasing decisions

A buyer buys to satisfy a need. That need consists of a mixture of objective and subjective parts. Objective needs include the need to eat, the need to get from A to B, the need to manufacture an end product at a certain cost in order to sell it at the market price. Subjective needs are emotional ones such as prestige or security. These are typified by such things as a wish to be seen to buy products that show you are well off.

The mix of objective and subjective needs will vary considerably from market to market. In the case of consumer goods, buyers are concerned largely with subjective needs such as emotional satisfaction, although they will also consider objective needs such as quality and price. An example is the 'own brand' consumer product marketed by large supermarkets. Unless the quality is similar to the quality of the branded product, consumers will not buy it even if it is cheaper. Luxury foods are purchased almost exclusively for emotional reasons. The same is true of luxury cars.

Industrial buyers will make their purchasing decision mainly on the basis of objective considerations – product performance, price, delivery and the quality of manufacture. There will however, also be subjective considerations such as the image of the product and the confidence they have in the company and the salespeople they are dealing with. Where products and prices are similar, subjective emotional considerations will decide which product is purchased. This choice will be influenced considerably by the information that the company gives and the manner in which it is presented.

Figure 6.2 shows how objective and subjective needs influence purchasing decisions for consumer goods, industrial goods and services.

FIGURE 6.2   The effect of 'needs' on purchasing decisions

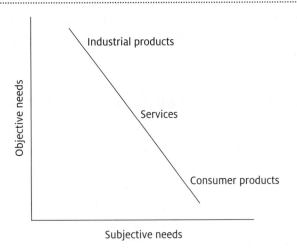

It follows that although personal contact selling can influence the client's subjective as well as objective considerations, it is more effective in industrial selling where objective considerations and technical understanding of the product have greater importance. The buyer of a fast sports car is more likely to have been influenced by the prestige of the product and media advertising than by the salesperson in the showroom who is only reinforcing the advertising message.

The influence of product characteristics on distribution channels

The characteristics of the product that you are selling will have a considerable influence on the mix of marketing channels that you select. Figure 6.3 shows how these product characteristics influence the choice between direct selling and distribution selling. The number of levels of channels of distribution will also affect prices because of the level of discounts that will need to be built into the price structure.

FIGURE 6.3   The influence of product characteristics on distribution channels

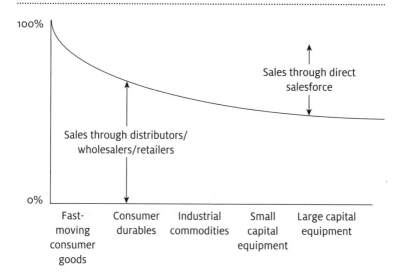

Direct sales

In a perfect world, direct selling with the salesperson face to face with the customer would give a company the maximum possibility of getting the message across and closing the sale. In the real world however, this is just not cost effective for large and medium-sized companies, who all employ a mixture of direct and indirect sales techniques. Small local businesses, however, only have the option of direct selling either in person or by phone. (In most cases the 'salesperson' is the owner or partner in the business.)

The advantages of personal selling are:

- It allows two-way communication between the buyer and seller. The buyer can ask questions about the product or service, and the salesperson can provide information in response to these questions.
- The salesperson can tailor the presentation to the individual needs of the customer. The sales message is personalized.
- The salesperson comes to know and be known by the customers.
- The salesperson can negotiate directly on price, delivery, discounts.
- The salesperson can close the sale.
- The salesperson can monitor customer satisfaction levels.

Distributors

Distribution channels for consumer goods

In consumer goods industries, distributors could be retailers, wholesalers or even companies that sell to wholesalers. In consumer markets it is usually the manufacturer who carries out the advertising campaigns to make the customer aware of the product. This is often the only way that the manufacturer can get its product message over to the consumer. The wholesale/retail system means that the manufacturer can deal with a smaller number of accounts and make larger individual deliveries of products. Because wholesalers and retailers hold stock the manufacturer has less need to do so. The manufacturer also uses their knowledge of the market and customer contacts.

The manufacturer gives the wholesaler a trade discount. This is a discount from the price list. In most cases the discount is substantial because it has to cover the distributors' costs of stocking, buying in bulk, redistributing to retailers or end-users and, of course, their profit. So although the manufacturer saves the cost of direct selling, this is partially offset by the discount that it has to give to the distributors. There would also normally be quantity discounts that would be offered to distributors who order in large quantities.

The distribution channels available for consumer goods are shown in Figure 6.4.

FIGURE 6.4 Distribution channels for consumer goods

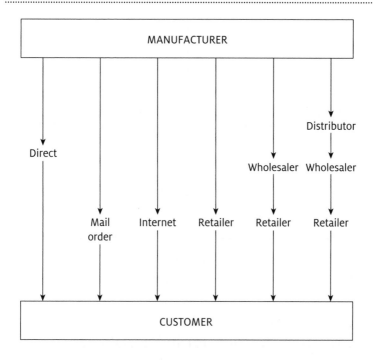

Distribution channels for services

For services the situation is different. There is no product on the shelf and so there is no requirement for wholesalers and retailers. The company supplying the service may sell it direct to the end-user or through an intermediary. The intermediary could be a commission agent, such as a travel agent or accommodation bureau, or a franchise-holder in the case of businesses offering on-site windscreen replacement, car-scratch repair or in many of the fast-food chains.

Figure 6.5 shows distribution channels for services.

FIGURE 6.5   Distribution channels for services

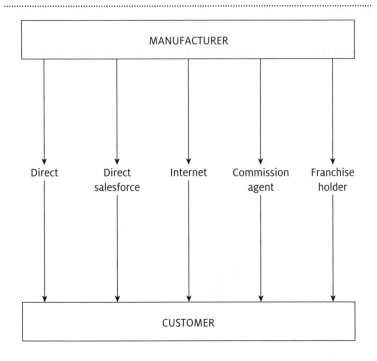

Distribution channels for industrial goods

For industrial goods, it is not usual to use wholesale/retail outlets like those used for consumer goods. Direct sales to customers generally make up a larger proportion of sales than with consumer goods, but the use of commission agents and distributors is widespread. In the United States these commission agents are often called 'manufacturers' reps'. The most common distinction is that a distributor holds stock and an agent or rep does not. Figure 6.6 shows distribution channels for industrial goods.

Most industrial manufacturers have a direct salesforce. With industrial goods there will often be 'key accounts' that are serviced differently from smaller customers. Commission agents act on behalf of a number of manufacturers of different but related products. The order is normally placed on the manufacturer by the customer and

FIGURE 6.6 Distribution channels for industrial goods

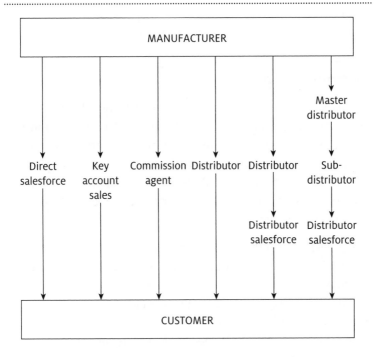

a commission is paid to the agent. A distributor takes over the selling role of the manufacturer, and most distributors will have their own salesforce dealing with customers. A distributor would normally be expected to hold enough stock to service the geographical area for which it is responsible. It may be an exclusive or a non-exclusive distributor. In large geographical areas master distributors would have their own sub-distributors. In export markets, sales in conjunction with commission agents or through distributors are the most common methods. Most distributors sell a range of products, so a product will not get the exclusive treatment through a distributor's salesforce that it would through a company's own salesforce.

A direct salesforce can be structured:

● by product;
● by area;

- by industry;
- by account.

Distributors can also be appointed on the same basis.

Telemarketing

Telemarketing involves selling and marketing by telephone rather than by direct physical contact. Generally, it has been found that telemarketing is most effective when it supplements the field sales-force activity rather than completely replacing it. It is cost effective because 40 to 50 telephone calls can be made per day whereas a rate of 6 to 10 personal visits per day is normal for direct sales calls. The main advantages of telemarketing are:

- The cost is lower than for a direct salesforce.
- It frees up the salesperson's time by reducing routine calling activity.
- It increases frequency of customer contact.
- It allows dormant accounts to be revived.
- In some cases it can be farmed out to a professional telemarketing company.

The types of telemarketing services available have expanded greatly in recent years. There are now a wide range of companies specializing in business-to-business (B2B) and business-to-customer (B2C) tele-marketing. Services offered include:

- lead generation;
- database maintenance;
- data collection;
- customer relations;
- prospecting;
- sales;
- customer retention.

You can even use a telemarketing company to assist your salesforce directly by finding out the right person to contact in a company and then making an appointment for your salesperson to call.

Currently, telemarketing uses telephone landlines. This is set to change within the next decade. Before the year 2000, virtually all telephone users had a landline, even though the use of mobile phones was increasing. By 2009 about 12 per cent of households in the UK and more than 20 per cent of households in the United States had no landline and only a mobile phone. Some analysts estimate that by 2015 the majority of households will have only mobile phones and that the last landline will be switched off in about 2025.

Websites

The internet provides companies with a major sales channel for all types of products. Online purchasing continues to grow at an amazing rate.

A 2008 report on e-commerce by the market research company Mintel showed that annual online sales in the UK in 2007 were worth £12.8 billion and were forecast to grow to £40 billion by 2012. According to the report, the move to purchasing online has been faster in the UK than in other European markets and the UK online market is worth 40 per cent more than the market in Germany and more than double the online market in France. By 2010, online sales accounted for 10 per cent of all UK retail sales.

The impact of the internet on prices

It has long been said that the two main effects of the internet on businesses are to drive down prices and to force uncompetitive companies out of business. The reality is not quite so clear-cut. With regard to prices, the internet works more as a mechanism that reduces the cost of getting information about products and prices. Customers who want to buy some electrical item, for example, no longer have to visit several local shops to compare prices. They can find out the average and lowest price of the item online. They can buy it online or, if they want to view the item, can still go into their local electrical superstore. If it is much more expensive there, they can still opt to buy online. So the main effect of the internet in this case is to make it more difficult for retailers to sell overpriced goods and to lead to a lower variation in prices and through that a lower level of price.

The impact of the internet on industry structures

A study by economists at the University of Chicago, published in the *Economic Journal* in June 2010, looked at the impact of e-commerce on three industries – bookshops, travel agencies and new-car dealerships. It concluded that in all three cases the growth of online shopping didn't just affect prices; it also changed the structure of the industry. As you might expect, the main change was that larger companies grew and some small ones went out of business. But the study also suggests that, although people who just want lower prices will go to the larger companies, small companies in the same industry can grow if they meet a specific need or offer a particular service or benefit.

It is easier to sell products online if they are easy to store, pack and dispatch. The US internet grocer Webvan found that out to its cost, when it collapsed 10 years ago. If Amazon gets a glut of orders, it can just ship some of the goods a few days later. Online grocery firms cannot do that – the goods may be perishable and customers want them when they need them. This goes some way to explain why, according to the research company Verdict, online sales accounted for only about 5 per cent of the UK grocery market in 2010, whereas they accounted for 10 per cent of total UK retail sales.

Ordinary website or e-commerce site?

I think it is clear that all companies need a website. The website needs to be well constructed and easy to navigate so that customers will use it and will come back to it. Small companies can have a website that is as good and comprehensive as those of their larger competitors. Any website will be a channel to market, because it will pass information to your customers in the same way that direct sales or telemarketing can. But not all companies need to take orders on their website and not every company needs to have a true e-commerce site. If your product is easy to store, pack and despatch, an e-commerce site is likely to benefit you. But, particularly in service industries, it may be necessary to provide individual quotations for individual jobs or projects. The details of the enquiry can be taken on the website through the 'contact us' page, but a separate quotation would then need to be prepared and e-mailed to the customer.

E-mail/e-marketing

E-marketing has brought about big changes in marketing tactics. It is relatively cheap and has the potential for reaching large numbers of customers. E-mail is the perfect vehicle to build lifetime relationships with customers.

Permission marketing

There are a large number of e-marketing companies that can supply permission-based technology to help businesses communicate and build or add to their existing database of potential and existing customers, creating targeted direct e-marketing campaigns with information and offerings specific to each customer's interests. Permission marketing can turn online visitors into lifetime customers by allowing regular communication with both existing and prospective customers. Giving consumers total control of messages they receive is the future of direct marketing on the internet. Permission marketing is the ideal solution to personalize relationships and secure continued customer support.

With opt-in e-mail, responses (5 to 15 per cent) are far greater than those from banner advertising (0.5 per cent) or traditional direct mail (1 to 3 per cent). In addition to a greater response rate, a direct e-mail marketing campaign costs only a fraction of the cost of more traditional methods of marketing. E-mail bulletins can even track how many users open the e-mails, and what if anything they click on in the bulletin. This is far more effective at collating customer information than direct mail.

E-mail list software

E-mail list software is set up with a server that is used to receive e-mail. The servers that are used to receive e-mail responses from e-mails sent out to a business e-mail list are designed to carry out particular tasks depending on the commands that are sent to them. 'Announcement lists' can be used to send one-way messages to consumers. These messages would contain information (such as special sales offers) that the company wants to inform its customer base about. These e-mails are worded in such a way as to make it clear that they do not require a response. If a customer on the e-mail list wants to unsubscribe from the list, the software will automatically do this, without the installer of the software having to do anything. This eliminates time lost by the business having to deal with the request personally. Some companies also set up 'discussion lists'. The subscribers to a 'discussion list' create a discussion group that makes comments on a particular range of topics that are of interest to the company.

If you are new to e-mail marketing it is sensible to consult a professional e-mail marketing company to help you plan your campaign. They will be able to provide you with opt-in e-mail lists that are relevant to your business and will also be able to help you to set up and manage your e-mail campaign. Once the campaign is underway, they will also be able to provide you with analysis and data reporting.

Viral marketing

Most e-mail marketing companies are also skilled in viral or 'word of mouth' marketing. Viral marketing means using techniques to get the recipients to do your marketing for you by forwarding your message to their friends and colleagues. Viral marketing can help you to grow your opt-in e-mail list, increase your brand exposure and also drive more traffic to your website. But creating a viral e-mail marketing campaign that will work requires a thorough understanding of the principles and is a job for an expert, so make sure that the company that you use has a good track record in this area.

Direct mail

Direct mail includes the mail-order business and the use of mailshots. Mailshots involve sending information on a specific product by mail to potential customers on a mailing list. They rely for their success on the accuracy of the mailing list used, and a small return rate (1–3 per cent) is considered quite normal. Direct Marketing Lists (**www.direct-marketing-lists.co.uk**) is one of the UK's largest suppliers of business and consumer mailing lists. They have a UK business database with over 3 million records and can provide mailing lists targeted by company size, industry, SIC code, area and a number of other criteria. Their consumer information is even more extensive with a comprehensive list of 37 million consumers with profiled information. They can provide custom-built mailing lists compiled using over 300 different profiles, which can include wealth, housing type, rateable value and general lifestyle factors. On their website they have a useful UK postcode map that you can download or print off.

Mailshots are still very popular, because small items or samples can be sent with the mailshot – something that is not possible with e-mail. But in many cases they are being superseded by e-mailshots on the grounds of cost and efficiency.

Physical distribution, warehousing and factory location

Your physical distribution involves not only the holding of stock, but also communicating within your distribution network and the way that your product is packaged for distribution. The proximity of the factory to its markets is more important with high-bulk/low-value goods than with sophisticated capital goods, but stocking at the factory, at warehouses or logistics centres is an important part of distribution strategy that will determine whether you can give as good a service as your competitors – or better.

As far as distribution is concerned, customer service relates to the level of availability of the product to the customer. Distribution is about getting the product to the right place (for the customer) at the right time. Theoretically you want to offer your customers 100 per cent availability of the product. In practice this is not possible. It is necessary to find a balance between the costs and benefits involved. The costs of extra availability cannot exceed the extra revenue that will be gained as a result.

Examples of strategies for distribution

Typical strategies and tactics for distribution are shown below.

Distribution

Strategy – change channels

Tactics:

- Set up own distribution direct to stores.
- Change distributor for area.
- Increase own sales coverage.
- Expand online shop.
- Increase number of warehouses for product.
- Reduce to use of only one large warehouse.

Strategy – improve service

Tactics:

- Set up national service network.
- Arrange service through major company with service centres throughout the area.

Examples

Below, we consider the marketing channels and physical distribution used by our sample companies and the changes and additions that they have decided to make.

The Pure Fruit Jam Company currently uses the following:

Marketing channels

The Pure Fruit Jam Company does not consider telemarketing or direct mail as these are not applicable channels for its type of product. It uses a mix of direct sales (to the wholesale buyers) and distribution (distributors sell to the small retailers). It carries out limited nationwide advertising of the products to support these channels. It is in the process of expanding its website to allow orders to be placed directly for gift packs and specialist products.

Physical distribution

The company manufactures its product in one factory only. It has a contract with a haulage contractor to deliver the product to major wholesalers, distributors and large retailers. The company has an integrated live computer database showing stocks at all these warehouses at all times. The product is packed in boxes – 30 jars to a box. The boxes are packed 12 to a pallet and shrink wrapped on the pallet.

For export markets The Pure Fruit Jam Company uses local distributors in individual countries. The product is packed in the same way as for delivery in the UK market.

Proposed changes/additions

The Pure Fruit Jam Company intends to expand its website to allow online purchases. It will also add Stats 2.0 web analytics software. It intends to expand its distribution outlets in the North of England and Scotland and to set up a distribution deal for its mini-pots range for the hotel trade. For export markets, it will continue to expand distribution – particularly in North America.

Quality Car Hire uses the following:

Marketing channels

Like most small regional businesses, Quality Car Hire uses direct selling. A lot of its business comes in because of 'word of mouth' recommendation and adverts in the local press and *Yellow Pages*. Much of its business is repeat business from existing customers. It has a website, but this is rather basic.

Physical distribution

Since Quality Car Hire keeps its cars at its two sites, physical distribution is not a problem.

Proposed changes/additions

Quality Car Hire intends to do more with the internet. It intends to expand its website and to add a 'contact us' section to allow potential customers to ask for a quote and check availability of a particular car for a particular date. It will be adding web analytics software to its website and it will use information gained to prepare targeted e-mails to specific customers with special offers. Targeted viral or 'word of mouth' marketing works very well for small businesses. It works on the basis that it is only human nature when you hear of a good deal to want to share it with others. So Quality Car Hire will be using targeted mailshots and e-mailshots.

The Gear Pump Company uses a different mix of marketing channels.

Marketing channels

The Gear Pump Company uses a mixture of direct sales (to large key accounts and contracting companies) and distributors (who hold stock of pumps and spares). It has recently started to use telemarketing to follow up dormant accounts. It has also set up an online shop on its website.

Physical distribution

The company manufactures pumps at its factory in the South of England and holds a stock of components and spare parts at the factory. It does not stock finished pumps and only supplies to order. The company's distributors operate on a discount level of 30 per cent from the company's list price and this finances the stocks of equipment that they hold in stock. The company uses local haulage contractors for deliveries of finished goods. More urgent deliveries are made using nationwide overnight services such as DHL, UPS and TNT. The company operates a materials resource planning (MRP) system with a computer database that includes order processing and invoicing. In addition the company operates a computer database for its distribution network and can advise distributors where they can find a component (with another distributor) if they do not have it in stock. With the agreement of their distributors, the company is making this database accessible to all distributors via its website. (This part of the website will be restricted and will only be accessible to authorized company and distributor personnel, who will have to log in individually.)

Proposed changes/additions

The Gear Pump Company intends to expand its website and will add web analytics software. It has its highest sales in the South of England, where it is based and in the Midlands and the North of England – where the company's distribution is strong. Its sales in Wales, Scotland and Northern Ireland are minimal. It is in the process of appointing a new distributor for Scotland and will be evaluating and possibly replacing its distribution in Wales and Northern Ireland.

Summary

- Distribution encompasses marketing channels, physical distribution and customer service.
- You need to be sure that you are using the best mix of the available marketing channels to sell your product.
- The characteristics of the product will influence the mix of marketing channels used.
- In consumer goods industries, distributors could be retailers, wholesalers or even companies that sell to wholesalers.
- For services there is no product on the shelf and so there is no requirement for wholesalers and retailers.
- For industrial goods direct sales to customers make up a larger proportion of sales than with consumer goods, but the use of commission agents and distributors is widespread.
- Although small local companies use only direct sales, most larger companies use a mix of direct sales and distribution through distributors, wholesalers, retailers and the like.
- Telemarketing involves selling and marketing by telephone rather than by direct physical contact. It is most effective where it supplements field salesforce activity rather than completely replacing it.
- Mailshots are still popular, but in many cases they are being superseded by e-mailshots on the grounds of cost and efficiency.
- E-marketing is the perfect vehicle to build lifetime relationships with customers. Viral marketing can help you to grow your opt-in e-mail list, increase your brand exposure and also drive more traffic to your website.
- The internet provides companies with a major sales channel for all types of product and online purchasing is growing at an amazing rate.
- It is easier to sell products online if they are easy to store, pack and dispatch.

Chapter seven
Advertising and sales promotion

In addition to personal selling, getting your message across to your customers involves the use of advertising and sales promotion.

Advertising

Advertising operates at three levels – it informs, persuades and reinforces.

- It informs potential customers about the company and its products. This is the creation of awareness.
- It advises customers of the benefits of the products and tells them why they should buy these products rather than other ones. It creates the desire to buy or own the product. This is the stage of persuasion.
- It reinforces existing positive attitudes in existing customers.

Advertising to *inform* normally relates to the promotion of new products and services. Advertising to *persuade* and *reinforce* is what most people understand as advertising.

Direct advertising is expensive and needs to be targeted effectively. There is no point in advertising a local car wash on national television. This is obvious, but there are many pitfalls that are not so obvious.

The expansion of satellite and cable television, commercial radio and the internet have dramatically changed the mix of national advertising. Much television advertising has migrated from free-to-air broadcasters to the pay-TV channels. Newspapers have seen even greater falls in advertising spending than television. The Newspaper Association of America reported that US print and online advertising fell by nearly 35 per cent between the first quarter of 2008 and the middle of 2010. Newspaper advertising is also moving online, but in many cases this is not to newspapers' websites. It is being taken by search engines. The classified-ad market has collapsed as it moves to free-listing websites.

National advertising

Because advertising on television and in the national press is very expensive, most television and national press advertising relates to consumer goods with large annual sales, or services such as banking and insurance from large companies. Where industrial advertising does take place in these media, it is mainly corporate image advertising for large companies such as Shell, British Gas and Unilever.

Consumer goods companies can easily get marketing information relating their products (or equivalent products) to the types of people that buy them. Companies selling advertising space also provide details of reader or viewer breakdown. The National Readership Survey (**www.nrs.co.uk**) provides up-to-date readership information for newspapers, general magazines and women's magazines. It covers 260 titles and provides the data by social class, by age and by sex. This information allows companies to decide which publications are best for advertising quality cars like Rolls Royce or Porsche and which are best for advertising investment schemes for the over 65s or mortgage deals for the under 25s.

Similar information is also readily available for regional television viewing areas such as Anglia, Meridian, Granada and Tyne Tees.

Local advertising

Local advertising includes newspapers, free newspapers and local commercial radio. It can also include local cinema advertising and outdoor advertising. Advertising in local newspapers has suffered as much as in national newspapers. The classified-ad market has been decimated by the move online, including the growth of free listings websites. Classified-ad magazines like *The Friday Ad* now have an online version that is continually updated, whereas the printed version of the magazine only appears once a week.

There has been an upsurge in the growth of local commercial radio over the last decade, and radio advertising is a good way for local businesses to get themselves known. Radio advertising is much less expensive than television advertising and, as discussed in Chapter 5, it is not restricted to indoor audiences but can be listened to in the car or on a portable device. It is important to remember that most people listen to the radio while doing other things so your advert will rely on repetition. If you are considering advertising on local or national radio you will need to research the market, the type of audience, the extent of the coverage and the cost per listener. You can get this by contacting a particular radio station. But if you are only at the stage of wondering if radio advertising might help you, I suggest that you contact the Radio Advertising Bureau (**www.rab.co.uk**).

Local cinema advertising offers a captive audience for your adverts. You need to ask the cinema for audience profiles and examples of satisfied customers. Depending on your product, you may want to target particular films or certain types of films.

National and local directories

There are a number of national and local trade directories that sell advertising space. Local directories include *Yellow Pages* (**www.yell. com**) and *Thomson Local* (**www.thomsonlocal.com**). They offer companies a free listing of their details but sell advertising space at the same time. They also have an online version of their directories. *Thomson Local* offers nectar points to both users and advertisers as a further incentive for them to use the service. National directories include Kompass (**www.kompass.co.uk**) – which also has overseas versions of its website and claims to have 'an online database of 2.7 million, high-quality, locally sourced company profiles from over 60 countries that is accessible in over 25 languages' and Kelly's (**www.kellysearch.com**). There are other more recently established business-to-business indexes, such as Approved Index (**www.approvedindex.co.uk**). Approved Index was set up by Reed Business Information in 2004. It offers free listing, but also a service where you register to pay for specific leads on a pay-per-lead basis.

Small and local businesses, particularly service companies, tend to advertise in local directories. *Thomson Local* and *Yellow Pages* both produce local town or area directories that are available in printed form and delivered to every household in the area, so having a listing and also an advert in these directories is important for businesses that only operate locally. The advertising in these local directories is also moving more and more online and in 2008 the *Yellow Pages* website **www.yell.com** accounted for 29 per cent of its UK sales and the number of advertisers in the printed directories fell by 14 per cent to 335,000.

Thomson Local has a free guide to advertising your business locally, which you can download from their website. This guide includes a list of six tips for Print Directory Advertising:

- Grab people's attention – tell people what is special about your services.
- Use an eye-catching header – make sure that you stand out from the local competition.
- A picture paints a thousand words – people read from left to right, so put a picture on the left of your advert.
- Your advert is your shop window – create the right image and give a strong visual message in your advert.
- People want to know that you are reliable – if you have been established for a long time, put it in your advert.
- Don't forget – include your location and logo – make sure your advert has a strong border, and is well spaced out. Don't clutter your advert.

In addition to running a business and online directory, *Thomson Local* also offers a wide range of direct marketing services including setting up company websites, search engine optimization (SEO) and products to help target potential customers using direct mail, tele-marketing and e-mail marketing.

Outdoor advertising

Outdoor advertising is the fastest-growing traditional advertising medium in the UK, with revenue totalling £938 million in 2008 and accounting for 9.9 per cent of UK advertising spending. There are a number of different types of outdoor advertising. These include:

- *Roadside*: static billboards, banners, phone kiosks.
- *Transport*: buses, taxis, lorries, railways (trains and stations), airports.
- *Retail sites*: shopping centres, supermarkets.

Static adverts rely on location for effectiveness, so you need to check the sites before booking the space. The location of most outdoor advertising sites mean that a large but untargeted audience could see it.

To decide if outdoor advertising is suitable for advertising your product you can get information from the Outdoor Advertising Association (OAA – **www.oaa.org.uk**).

Industrial goods

The advertising of industrial and capital goods uses much narrower and more specific outlets such as industry specific magazines or websites. The products are generally aimed at a much smaller number of end-users and advertising will normally be placed in industry-specific technical magazines.

A company selling equipment used in food production would advertise in magazines such as *Food Manufacture*. A company selling equipment used in the pulp and paper industry would advertise in *PPI* (Pulp and Paper International). Each industry and each industry sector has its own technical press and their advertising departments can normally provide details of circulation by number, area and type of reader (plant manager, engineer, management, etc).

Repeat advertising is more effective than one-off advertisements. The same advert repeated every week or every month in a limited number of outlets is more effective than different one-off adverts in a wide range of outlets.

Industrial companies can also target their advertising expenditure by using one of the wide range of independent websites that have been established in recent years for specific types of industrial equipment (pumps and valves, vacuum equipment, mixing equipment) or industries (pulp and paper, chemical manufacturing, water and waste treatment). Most of these websites offer a listing that includes company and product details for a nominal amount, and also offer advertising.

Online advertising

In the first half of 2009 the UK became the first major economy where advertisers spent more on internet advertising than on television. Figures from the Internet Advertising Bureau (IAB – **www.iabuk.net**), which is the trade association for online advertising, showed that the internet accounted for 23.5 per cent of all advertising money spent in the UK. This compared with 21.9 per cent for television advertising. The IAB figures showed that 60 per cent of the total internet spend was on search advertising on websites such as Google, about 22 per cent on online classified advertising and only 18 per cent on online display advertising, such as banners on websites. The IAB believes that internet advertising could continue to grow to reach about 30 per cent of the UK's total advertising spend.

Websites

If you want to do any advertising online, you need to have a website. Most online advertising (search advertising) is geared to directing people to your website. In 2008 the British Market Research Bureau stated that 80 per cent of internet users use the internet as their preferred method of finding information about goods and services. Your website is a permanent shop window that is available 24 hours a day seven days a week.

Affiliate marketing

This uses affiliate programmes or arrangements in which an online merchant website pays affiliate websites a commission to send them traffic through the use of links. Recruiting affiliates is a cost-effective way for a company to get its products known online. It results in the company's brand being advertised on a range of different websites, but the company only ends up paying for the click-throughs or sales. The best example of an affiliate strategy is Amazon (**www.amazon.com**), which is currently estimated to have over half a million affiliates. The affiliate can link to the merchant's site by means of a text link, a banner link or a search box – the type of link will depend on the type of website and the type of product or service being sold. Payment for the goods sold can be made as 'pay per sale', where the merchant pays the affiliate a percentage of the purchase price or a set fee per transaction, 'pay per click', where the affiliate is paid based on the number of visitors who click on the link to the merchant's site, or 'pay per lead', where the affiliate is paid based on the number of visitors who sign up to the merchant's website.

Social media websites

Social media websites such as Facebook and YouTube are trying to increase their advertising revenues. Both provide full details of advertising possibilities on their websites. Facebook allows you to select your audience by location, age and interests and to test out simple image and text-based ads. It suggests that companies advertising on Facebook can advertise their own web page, create demand for their products by creating relevant adverts or publicize an event such as a product launch or company anniversary. Payment is either by 'pay per click' or by 'impression' (visitors see the ad, whether they click on it or not). You can set a daily budget that can be adjusted up or down at any time. YouTube offers a YouTube Media Kit that enables you to visit its own Advertising Brand Channel to learn the basics of launching a successful marketing campaign with it, and also offers YouTube Self-Service Ads. Advertising on social media websites should only be undertaken as part of a coordinated social media strategy.

Banners and display advertising

Display 'banners' or banner ads were the first major method used for online advertising, and in 2002 they had the bulk of the market. But by 2009, this had dropped to less than 20 per cent of internet advertising as 'pay per click' or 'keyword' advertising became the predominant force. At the time of writing, display banners still have merit and are good for special offers or for reinforcing a brand. Banner ads are small adverts that normally come in various rectangular forms. They appear on websites and serve as a link directly to the advertiser's website: when you click on the banner your browser instantly redirects you to that site. The popularity of banner ads is in part due to the fact that they are simple to produce and publish. They are also highly measurable. Depending on the ad and the product or service, advertisers can calculate the cost per sale – this is the amount of advertising money that is spent to make one sale.

By definition a banner ad has to be posted on someone else's website. It is best to use an agency that specializes in the networking of banner ads to make the necessary arrangements.

Pay per click (PPC) or keyword advertising

Search engines and many websites (including social networking sites such as Facebook) carry small adverts with embedded URLs. When someone clicks on these adverts, the company that put them there is charged. This is now the preferred method of online advertising and has been growing at a remarkable rate. Unlike traditional advertising, 'pay per click' is user activated. Users like it, because it costs them nothing and they only use it if there is something that attracts them. The advantage of pay per click for advertisers is that they only pay for the actual click through to their site. With other methods of advertising, both on and offline, you have no guarantee as to how much you may have to pay to attract each visitor. It is a fact that visitors who click through to your site through a search engine are quite likely to purchase products, because these visitors are actively looking for the type of product that you are offering.

A PPC ad is usually a text ad that is placed near to a search result. In theory the advertiser does not pay for the placement, because technically the listings are free. The advertiser only pays for each click (which means each visitor) that they receive from the search engine listing. When the site visitor clicks on to the ad, the advertiser is charged a set fee, which could be anything from a few pence to several pounds depending on the popularity of the search term and which search engine is being used. When you set up a PPC advertising campaign, you can usually set a maximum amount of spend per day or a total overall spend for your campaign, so that you know what your maximum spend could be.

There are three main types of PPC advertising engines:

- *Keyword*: advertisers using these engines have to bid on keywords or phrases. If a user carries out a search using a particular word or phrase, the list of advertiser links appear in order with the highest bidder first.
- *Product or price comparison*: product or price comparison engines let advertisers provide feeds of their product databases. When users search for a product, the links to different advertisers for that product appear, with the advertisers who paid more at the top of the list. There is a facility to let the user sort by price to see the lowest-priced product and then click on that link.
- *Service*: service engines let advertisers provide feeds of their service databases. It functions in a similar way to product comparison.

There are a large number of search engines available, including Google, Yahoo, MSN live and ASK. There are also 'metasearch' engines that incorporate traffic from numerous other search engines and online sources, and small, niche search engines that specialize in one or more categories or topics of interest. The most popular service is Google Adwords. Google can deliver more from PPC than smaller search engines because it has the largest number of users of any search engine. Google tries to make it very easy for companies to use its Adwords service – it will even help you create a website if you don't have one. Adwords is a keyword-based product and Google say that all you have to do is:

- create your ad;
- choose your keywords;
- set the limit of your geographical coverage;
- set your budget.

So PPC advertising is very targeted – at a consumer looking for something that is quite specific. You can limit it to specific geographical regions to avoid paying for 'interest' clicks that are not likely to result in business. You only pay when someone clicks on your advert, but that means that your advert has to appear. You can improve the likelihood of that happening by bidding for keywords.

The main benefits of paid search advertising using PPC are:

- It can be set up and implemented very quickly, so you generate visits to your website very quickly.
- It is cost effective and you can control what you spend by setting up maximum daily budgets.
- You can pause your advertising campaign at any time.
- You get relevant and focused visitors.
- Companies like Google offer easy to use tools to track the return on your investment.
- Size doesn't matter – it is just as effective for small companies as for large ones.

Even though setting up and operating PPC advertising is quite straightforward, it can be time-consuming and complicated to manage properly. Many companies therefore decide to pay an expert to manage this service for them to make sure that they get the most out of their PPC advertising. A lot more detailed information about 'pay per click' advertising and the different search engines can be found at Pay Per Click Universe (**www.payperclickuniverse.com**).

Really simple syndication (RSS)

Although at an early stage, RSS is being used for private advertisements such as job adverts, information about apartment rentals as well as buying and selling goods.

Search engine optimization (SEO)

The huge increase in the number of companies operating and selling on the internet has dramatically increased the competition between companies to get visitors to their websites rather than to those of their competitors. When carrying out a web search, most people will only look at the first page of search results and often only at the top two or three results. So making sure that your site gets high up in the results is important to the success of your website. There are ways of improving your search engine ranking, and search engine optimization is the method of achieving this. Search engine optimization is a complex science and there is a lot of jargon that is difficult to understand, so it is better to use a specialist SEO company. Both the content and the HTML coding of a website are important in improving its search ranking, and an SEO company can modify both in such a way that it achieves a higher ranking in search engine listings for relevant terms relating to your product or service offering. It can also set up links to your site from other websites in your field of expertise. Using an SEO company can be a one-off cost for an initial optimization, or an ongoing consultancy. (Don't forget that as you move up the rankings, those that you displace will try to recover their ground.)

Planning your advertising campaign

You need to set objectives for your advertising campaign and these objectives must be realistic. You need to define both the audience that you wish to reach and why you need to reach them. A company that says 'we never know how successful our advertising is' is not planning or monitoring its advertising correctly and may be throwing money down the drain. You cannot measure the success of your advertising directly in sales, but there are many techniques for measuring the effectiveness of a campaign.

In consumer goods industries, the effect of advertising is often measured by carrying out consumer surveys. With industrial goods it is a matter of noting the number of responses or 'reader replies' from each advertisement in the technical press. With online advertising it is often much easier to measure the effectiveness of a campaign, because most systems for online advertising include their own systems for analysis.

If you are planning an advertising campaign you need to answer the following questions:

- Who are the target audience?
- What is your message?
- What response do you want to get from the target audience?
- How can you best get this response?
- What is the most cost-effective medium for your advertising?
- When should you advertise?
- How long should the advertising campaign be?
- How are you going to measure the results?
- How much money are you going to spend?

You need to tie in your advertising objectives with your marketing objectives. It is important to spend money on advertising in a logical way. If you are selling industrial equipment and you are budgeting to spend £30,000 on a campaign, you would not spend it on one television advert or a one-page advertisement in a major national newspaper. You would spend it over a 6–12-month period by advertising in a range of trade journals/magazines. Repeat advertising is more effective than one-off advertisements. As we noted earlier, the same advert repeated every week or every month in a limited number of outlets is more effective than different one-off adverts in a wide range of outlets.

Example

The Gear Pump Company is targeting the water industry. Table 7.1 shows an advertising schedule that it has prepared. The advertising schedule includes the annual cost of subscribing to the website **www.waterproducts.com**. This is a website that specializes in products used in the water and waste treatment industries. Descriptions of their individual products for the water industry are shown on the site and pdf files of their technical literature and data sheets can be downloaded from it. The site has a 'web analytics' system and can

TABLE 7.1 Press advertising schedule

ADVERTISING

Application: Water industry   Year: 20X6

MEDIA	No	Rate per insertion (£)	Total cost (£)	J	F	M	A	M	J	J	A	S	O	N	D
Water and Waste Treatment	2	1,800	3,600				X								X
Water Services	2	1,500	3,000						X						X
Water Bulletin	3	800	2,400			X					X				X
waterproducts.com	1	2,000	2,000	X	X	X	X	X	X	X	X	X	X	X	X
TOTAL COST			11,000												

provide the company with lists of users who visit the site and details of which of the companies' products they have looked at. The company will also be carrying out some targeted mail/e-mailshots and expanding its own website to include 'web analytics' for e-marketing.

A company selling consumer products such as chocolate or break-fast cereal would normally have a much wider spread of advertising coverage, but it would still be a coordinated campaign. Care would be taken to get the best mix of TV, press and poster advertising. If you consider that Nestlé sell a billion Kit Kat bars in the UK every year with a total value of nearly £200 million you can appreciate that advertising budgets for such products are likely to be many millions of pounds a year.

Sales promotion

Sales promotions are used by companies in both the consumer and industrial market, although the usage is much greater for consumer products. The amount spent on sales promotion in the UK is esti-mated to be in excess of £5 billion a year, making it similar in size to the expenditure on advertising. The Promotion Marketing Association suggests that in the United States spending on sales promotion is actually higher than spending on normal advertising.

The spectacular growth in the use of sales promotion dates from the late 1960s, and sales promotion expenditure in real terms in many markets has grown fivefold in that time. This reflects a change in Western economies, where there has been a change from 'pull' purchasing to 'push' selling. With the spread of supermarkets, hyper-markets and self-service outlets, there are now a huge number of brands of almost every product competing for the same consumer. So more inducement is necessary to get people to buy a particular product.

What is a sales promotion?

Sales promotion is a term used to describe promotional methods using specific short-term techniques to persuade the members of the target market to respond in a particular way. The reward is something of value to those responding. This can take the form of a reduction in the price of purchasing a product (eg a discount on the normal price, 'buy one get one free', 'three for the price of two') or the inclusion of additional value-added material (eg something more for the same price such as '20 per cent more for no extra charge').

A sales promotion must have the following elements:

- It must be a featured offer and not part of normal trade.
- The offer must give the customer some tangible advantage.
- It must be designed to achieve an increase in sales over a specific time period.

A sales promotion will normally contain one of the following catch-phrases – 'free', 'save' or 'win'.

The difference between sales promotion and advertising

Many people confuse sales promotions with advertising, but there are differences. Take the example of an energy company using an advert on television to offer respondents the chance of winning a pair of cup final tickets if they register their details on the company website and take part in a simple game. The advert itself on television is certainly advertising, but the offer of a game with a prize is considered to be a sales promotion. The key factors that determine whether something is a sales promotion or advertising are:

- Is the promotion only offered for a limited period of time? (In the case of the cup final example, there is clearly a closing date before the event itself takes place.)
- Does the customer have to perform some activity to be eligible to receive the reward? (In the case of the example, the customer has to log onto the company's website and take part in the game.)

The inclusion of a time constraint and an activity requirement show this example is a sales promotion.

Example

As well as being a major advertiser, Nestlé also spends large sums on sales promotion. In fact it even has a special promotional website just for its Kit Kat chocolate bars (**www.kitkat.co.uk**). At the time of writing it was running two sales promotions. The first one is called 'Cross Your Fingers' and offers a £1,000 prize every day. To enter, customers need to buy a promotional pack of Kit Kat and enter the code from the pack together with their contact details on the Kit Kat website. As an alternative, the customer can also enter the code via SMS using a mobile phone. 'Perfect Break' is a separate promotion with different promotional packs and prizes worth up to £10,000 that include weekend breaks, holidays for two in various parts of the world and sports-related holidays.

A sales promotion cannot take the place of advertising or selling and it cannot change long-term trends in the life of a product or brand. It can, however, encourage a consumer to behave more in line with the economic interests of the manufacturer. It can:

● increase volume sales in the short term;
● stimulate stock movement;
● encourage repeat purchase;
● increase customer awareness/loyalty/purchase frequency;
● increase market penetration of new products;
● bring forward buying peaks;
● dispose of old models before a new model is introduced.

Company loyalty cards

In the consumer goods industries, customer loyalty cards have become a major sales promotional tool that allows large stores, particularly supermarkets, to make targeted offers and promotions to individual customers. The use of the company loyalty card means that every time people shop, they provide data that indicate the pattern of their likely future purchasing decisions. This allows the supermarket to target those customers specifically with offers that are likely to appeal to them. In addition to sending vouchers through the post, most large supermarkets now have their system set up in a way that allows them to print off vouchers with offers at the same time that they print out your bill. These vouchers vary from '20p off' or '50p off' if you purchase a particular product within a week or 10 days to vouchers offering triple card points or '£6 off if you spend £60 on your next shop', again with a time limit of a week or 10 days. The purpose of these vouchers is to persuade customers:

- not to do their next major shop in a different supermarket and risk losing the value of the offer;
- to spend much more than the amount required to get the discount to make sure that they reach the target figure.

If you do your supermarket shopping online, you will also find that from time to time you receive vouchers for even larger discounts, but only if you shop in store. This is to make sure the supermarket can get you into the shop from time to time in the hope that you will impulse buy other products that you would not perhaps buy in an online shop.

Managing sales promotions

Sales promotions are often badly managed and regarded as just another advertising or general marketing expense. In fact, a sales promotion needs to increase the contribution to the company from the sales of the product in question. If a product has a contribution of £1, a sales promotion offering 10p off your next purchase needs to bring about a 10 per cent increase in sales just to make the same contribution. An increase of more than 10 per cent is necessary for the promotion to start to be successful.

In the same way that you need to set objectives for advertising campaigns, you also need to set your objectives for sales promotions.

Objectives for sales promotions could be:

- to increase sales by X per cent;
- to introduce a new product;
- to encourage repeat purchases;

- to combat competition;
- to move buying peaks;
- to increase sales out of season.

To be effective a sales promotion must have a well-defined but limited time span. If your product is always offered at a 10 per cent discount this will eventually become the market price.

Example

The Pure Fruit Jam Company decides to carry out a sales promotion for its gift packs. The gift packs include jars of specialist whisky or brandy-flavoured marmalades and most sales are in the run-up to Christmas. Sales are particularly low during the early summer months.

Objective: to stimulate sales of gift packs throughout the months of June, July and August when sales are traditionally low. It is expected that the promotion will double the value of goods sold over this period and that there will also be additional advantages to the company, which will be able to:

- continue production at normal rates;

- reduce stock costs;

- improve cash flow.

The promotion will involve the sale of gift packs in new special packaging. Customers can enter a competition to win a weekend break for two either in Scotland or in the Cognac region of France. Included in the weekend break will be a visit and tasting at either a whisky distillery in Scotland or a brandy distillery in France. To enter, customers need to register their details together with the code from the back of the pack on the company website. To promote the offer, the company will request stores to stock more of their gift packs, and in return it will provide free-of-charge special display boards and promotional posters. The company will also carry out a press and TV advertising campaign to support the promotion. The advantage of getting customers to register their details is that it gives the company a database of customers who may be interested in purchasing the company's more upmarket products.

Online sales promotions

Most e-commerce website packages offer a range of marketing tools, including sales promotional offerings. These usually include:

- gift certificates;
- gift wrapping;
- site promotions;
- sale items;
- volume discounts;
- membership points.

It is becoming common for small businesses to use viral or 'word of mouth' marketing concepts as one of their main methods of sales promotion. There are many specialist e-marketing companies that offer tailored packages to be used for this. Typically an offer might involve sending a customized e-mail message to subscribers of a mailing list, offering them a chance to win a prize, small gift certificate or even the chance to try out a product or service free of charge. The key to viral marketing is exposure. You want potential clients to visit your website and see what you have to offer. The prize is to make their visit worthwhile. Customized software allows you to select recipients who would be most likely to respond well to your product, based on stated preferences and mailing list subject matter. You can also personalize each message with each client's name.

Examples of strategies for advertising and sales promotion

Examples of strategies and tactics relating to advertising and sales promotion are shown below.

Strategy – change advertising

Tactics:

- increase advertising for the product in specific markets;
- start new advertising campaign;
- carry out mailshot/e-mailshot;
- update and expand website;
- add 'web analytics' for e-marketing;
- increase company image advertising.

Strategy – increase sales promotion

Tactics:

- offer limited time promotion with chance for participants to win prizes;
- introduce voucher scheme to encourage repeat purchase;
- offer incentive scheme to distributors.

Summary

- The purpose of advertising is to get a message across to your customers. It operates at three levels – it informs, persuades and reinforces ideas about your company and its products.
- Because advertising on television and in the national press is very expensive, most television and national press advertising relates to consumer goods with large annual sales, services such as banking and insurance, and image advertising by large companies.
- Most small businesses that operate locally or regionally use local advertising. The channels used include local newspapers, directories, free newspapers, commercial radio, cinema and outdoor advertising.
- The advertising of industrial and capital goods uses much narrower and more specific outlets such as industry-specific magazines or websites.

- In 2009 the UK became the first major economy where advertisers spent more on internet advertising than on television advertising. Sixty per cent of online advertising is spent on search advertising.

- Banner advertising was the first major method used for online advertising, but by 2009 'pay per click' or keyword advertising had become the predominant force. The most popular 'pay per click' service is Google Adwords.

- Making sure that your website ranks high up in the results of web searches is important to the success of your website. Search engine optimization (SEO) is the method that companies use to improve their search engine ranking.

- Advertising on social media websites should only be undertaken as part of a coordinated social media strategy.

- When planning an advertising campaign you need to set realistic objectives. You need to define both the audience you wish to reach and why you wish to reach them.

- Sales promotions are promotional methods that use short-term techniques to persuade members of a target market to respond in a particular way. The reward is something of value to those responding, such as 'buy one get one free'. Sales promotions are widely used for consumer goods.

- Sales promotions differ from advertising by including a time constraint and an activity requirement. The amount spent on sales promotion in the UK is similar to the amount that is spent on advertising.

Chapter eight
Promotional materials, presentations and exhibitions

The high quality that is necessary for both material preparation and printing means that even large companies with their own marketing and sales promotion department will use some outside help in the preparation of adverts, brochures and exhibition materials. Some companies may decide to manage the work themselves with the help of outside photographers, agencies and/or printers, but others may decide that it is more cost effective to let a sales promotion company handle the projects for them.

Sales literature

There are generally three levels of company/sales literature:

- *Corporate or image brochures*: very high quality, glossy.
- *Sales brochures*: high quality, glossy.
- *Data sheets*: functional, may or may not include photos.

The corporate brochure is a high-quality prestige document that is designed to tell your customers key information about your company. It usually includes a short history of the company, some detail of how it is structured and details of its key products. Above all, it is an 'image' brochure and its purpose is to transmit the image that the company wants to get over to its customers. It has to look good and has to include only quality photos and artwork. It is expensive to produce, to print and to reprint. For this reason many companies are now choosing to replace the corporate brochure by putting the same information on their website.

It is important to get your literature portfolio right. These are the documents that customers will read to get to understand more about your products, and are the documents that you want them to keep to refer to if they need your type of product in the future.

There are two ways to structure your literature portfolio. You can produce high-quality brochures for each product or group of products. These brochures would include all of the technical detail that your customers need as well as details of applications for the product, and would possibly also include endorsements of the product by key customers. The alternative is to have an overall sales brochure or a sales brochure for each family of products supported by individual data sheets for each individual product.

I am an advocate of having an overall brochure supported by data sheets. Sales brochures are quality printed documents that you cannot produce yourself. Data sheets are much more basic documents and many companies can produce and modify them in-house. The danger with having too much detail in a sales brochure is that it quickly becomes out of date. You don't want to be giving one to a customer and having to say: 'Oh by the way, the product shown on page 3 has now been replaced by a new model.' I find it much easier and much more cost effective to keep the brochure simple and to have all of the detail in the data sheets – typically a literature portfolio might consist of three product brochures, each supported by four or five data sheets.

Photography

Photographs are used in all aspects of sales promotion. They are used in adverts, sales brochures, data sheets and sales presentations, as well as on websites and in exhibitions. You need different types and different levels of quality for different purposes.

With the advent of digital photography, anyone can take a photograph anywhere. So for internal presentations it is possible to make some use of photographs taken by your own personnel in-house. It is also possible to get some photographs through your sales team. But remember that most customers are very sensitive about the taking of photographs on their premises and your sales personnel should never do this without first getting the customer's permission.

The quality of photographs that you take yourself may be good enough to use in a PowerPoint presentation, but will not be good enough to use in sales literature or for exhibitions. For this you need higher-resolution images taken by a professional photographer. You also need the expertise of the professional to get the angle, lighting and everything else right. The one thing that you do not do is use a local photographer who specializes in portraits and weddings.

If you have never used a professional photographer before, then seek advice, either from contacts that you have or from one of the sales promotion companies that you deal with.

Choose your photographer based on what type of shots you want. Think long term – you may require a shot of a piece of equipment now to use in a brochure, but next year you may want to use the same shot for an exhibition panel and need to be able to blow the photograph up to a size of $1m \times 1m$. Similarly, consider whether colour photos will suit all your needs or if you may need some to be available in both colour and black and white. Colour photos are used for most applications, but black and white photos are very useful to use in things like data sheets. A colour photo may well not look as good when printed in black and white unless the photographer was aware of that requirement when taking the shot.

Fees for photography vary widely, so get a quotation before going ahead and make sure that you understand what you are paying for. Remember that you will not own the photograph; under copyright law the owner of the copyright is the person who created it, in this case the photographer. Try to negotiate a price that allows you to use the photograph for a specific number of times in a range of media such as brochures, adverts and exhibition material. But don't forget that eventually the photo will be out of date and out of style, so don't pay a fortune to get the rights to use it for 10 years.

If you need a specific type of photograph to use in a brochure, such as a shot of a typical chemical plant or of cows in a milking parlour, it is cheaper to use a photographic library to get a suitable photograph than to commission a professional photographer. Photographic libraries hold collections of pictures under a wide range of different categories. Some will supply a catalogue on request, but many can be accessed directly over the internet and you can browse the catalogue online. Photo libraries can supply digital images in a range of resolutions from low to very high resolution. Most can also supply hard copy transparencies or prints for direct use in artwork. Details of photo libraries can be found from the British Association of Picture Libraries and Agencies (**www.bapla.org.uk**). It has an A–Z of picture suppliers and an A–Z of picture categories.

Online printing

For many companies, and particularly for small and medium-sized ones, the cost of printing company brochures and data sheets is a major expense. But what do you now use printed literature for? In the days before the internet, the only way that companies could provide their customers with quality printed information about their company and its products was by preparing and printing brochures and data sheets. There would be a large literature store and this material would be sent out to satisfy 'customer requests' resulting from advertising or exhibitions. Large quantities of brochures and data sheets would also be sent to various exhibitions. Companies would normally have a minimum of a company brochure and a range of product brochures and data sheets. Most companies still have these, although many have now dropped the 'company brochure' completely. But really the only place that hard copy literature still needs to be available is at exhibitions.

Many companies have recognized this and are now drastically cutting their literature printing costs by making their brochures and data sheets available as pdf files on their websites and encouraging potential customers to download the material they need and print it off themselves. The high-quality literature still needs to be prepared in the first place, so the origination costs have not been reduced, but the printing costs have. Many printing companies will now also keep your brochure in a digital format and print off an extra few hundred or few thousand copies whenever you require them. So it is not necessary to purchase a huge quantity to keep costs down and then to have the problem of storing them.

Presentations

Presentations make very effective sales tools and are also useful for training your sales team on all aspects of your business and products. No one can be an expert on absolutely everything, but good sales presentations help salespeople to get the best out of every sales call, even when unexpected topics are raised.

Nowadays, everyone uses overhead presentations, and I favour the use of the Microsoft Office software package with the PowerPoint presentation program.

PowerPoint is not a difficult package to get to grips with, although becoming an expert requires training and lots of hard work. Almost anyone can start to use PowerPoint and prepare basic presentations with just a little guidance.

Some tips when preparing and making a presentation

- Use large font sizes for the text.
- Use an easy to read typeface such as Times New Roman or Arial.
- Don't try to get too many lines of text on a slide – about 10 is ideal.
- Use introductory slides with key headings and follow these up with separate slides expanding each of these headings.
- Bring bullet points in one by one to avoid the audience trying to read the whole slide rather than listening to your presentation.
- Consider using a background colour to enhance the impact of your presentation.
- Prepare a 'slide master' or 'background template' with your company name and logo on it.

- Include horizontal lines top and bottom to give your slides an 'active area'.
- Enhance your presentation by importing tables or graphs from Microsoft Excel (if applicable).
- Import suitable photos into your slides (if applicable).
- You can copy an open web page onto a PowerPoint slide by pressing the 'Control' (ctrl) and 'Print Screen' (PrtSc) buttons together and then using the 'edit' and 'paste' functions in PowerPoint.

I have included below a few examples of PowerPoint slides prepared by our sample companies for use in their presentations.

FIGURE 8.1 Powerpoint template for use in company presentations

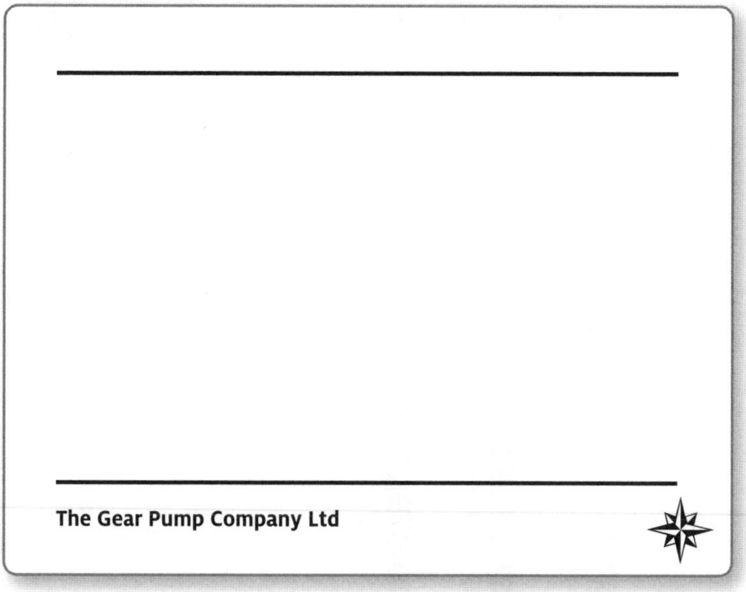

The Gear Pump Company Ltd

FIGURE 8.2   Slide with bullet points

GEAR PUMP TRAINING

Key Industries – Micro Gear Pumps

- Chemical/Petrochemical
- Water and Waste Water
- Pulp & Paper
- Food

The Gear Pump Company Ltd

FIGURE 8.3   Slide incorporating a bar chart imported from Excel

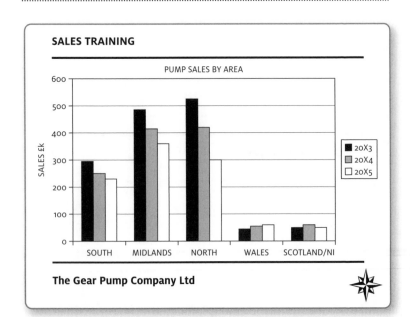

FIGURE 8.4   Slide combining a photograph and text
(photograph courtesy of Louise Westwood)

SALES MEETING 20X6

NEW JAR DESIGN

- Rustic shape
- Corners resist breakage
- Easy to open
- Two sizes
- Flat side for label

Pure Fruit

Exhibitions

Exhibitions can be a good showcase for your products. They vary from small local events to major national exhibitions or trade shows. Exhibitions are expensive and the reasons for attending must be carefully considered beforehand and the cost justified. The type of company you are will determine what is cost effective for you. If you are a small local organization, then only smaller local or regional exhibitions would be of interest. Industrial products are normally exhibited at exhibitions that are specific for that industry rather than general trade fairs. If you are participating in an overseas exhibition it is often possible to get government support, including grants. This is covered in detail in Chapter 11.

Why exhibit?

When you book a stand at an exhibition, it is important that you set clearly defined objectives that fit in with your overall marketing strategy. What is the purpose of attending the event? How would you define a successful outcome and how will you measure this?

So list your key aims for the exhibition. They could be to:

- cement and improve contact with key existing customers;
- continue discussions on XYZ project with customer;
- gain a set number of new potential customers;
- introduce and promote a new product;
- increase market share for existing products;
- assess the competition.

The size and design of the stand

In booking a stand, remember that size matters – both in terms of being able to properly exhibit the material that you want to display and also in terms of the impression that the stand will make on your customers and potential customers. Large companies often feel that they need to take larger stands to promote the 'right image'. Smaller companies can take small stands without it appearing that they are cutting costs or penny-pinching.

You need to think about the layout of the stand, both in terms of the displays and in terms of space to sit and talk to key customers. But size costs money, so this is an iterative process. How much space do I think I need? Approximately how much will this cost? Is this within our budget? (Or in many cases – can I afford this?)

Table 8.1 shows an example of how a company might put together an approximate cost for an exhibition stand at a major exhibition.

When you are booking a stand, most exhibition organizers will offer you the alternative of a basic stand or a more expensive 'shell stand'. The former is just the stand space and you will have to build your stand completely from scratch. The latter will include walls, a basic floor covering, possibly a ceiling and some basic lighting. It will also normally include a standard facia board with the stand

TABLE 8.1   Schedule of expenditure for a major exhibition

EXHIBITION COSTS
Name of exhibition: IWEX

Location: NEC Birmingham
Date: 6–8 November 20X6

Stand size: 64m² (8m × 8m)
Stand Contractor: Exhibition Contractors Ltd

COSTS	£
Stand space rental	10,000
Design, supply and build	12,000
Artwork, photographic panels	5,000
Rental of carpets, furniture, lights, phone, etc	3,000
Hotel bills/expenditure for stand staff	4,000
TOTAL	34,000

number and your company's name. So even with a shell stand, you still have a lot to supply yourself.

A small company taking a small amount of space can rent or buy a 'pop-up' stand from an exhibition stand supplier. This is a simple, portable design that looks professional and is inexpensive. Pop-up display stands have a collapsible frame that is quick and easy to put up and on which graphics can be displayed. For a larger stand there is really no option but to have one custom made.

As you can see in Table 8.1, the rental of the stand space, although significant, is often only about a quarter of your total costs of taking part in an exhibition. The other major expenditure will be the cost of a designer/contractor to design your stand and transport, erect and dismantle it. This is usually the largest expense so you may decide to do this yourself, but even so you will almost certainly need to prepare some new display material. For most companies it is cost effective to use a stand designer/contractor even if you will be including some of your own equipment models and visual display materials. Exhibition contractors know their job. They will get on with the job and leave you to get on with selling. Always get quotes from several designers/contractors, and always get the contractor you select to do several designs.

There is no point in exhibiting if you don't get the right people (customers and potential customers) to your stand. And there is no point in getting the right people to your stand if you do not follow up on their visit in order to generate new business. So you need to have a media plan in place to support the exhibition. Depending on the target group, the message you want to get across and the budget that you have available, this can vary. Below is an example of a media plan that you could adapt to suit your own circumstances:

Before the exhibition

Objective:

- To get the right visitors to come to your stand.

Actions:

- Complete company and product entries in exhibition catalogue and supporting online material.
- Carry out selective trade press advertising with reference to the exhibition stand (where relevant).
- Carry out direct mail/e-mailshot.
- Send out personal exhibition invitations to key customers/ potential customers.

During the exhibition

Objective:

- To get the right visitors to come to your stand.
- To support the visit.

Actions:

- Provide supplementary advertising in the exhibition catalogue and newsletter (at major exhibitions, newsletters are often circulated and updated daily).

- Provide press kits.
- Hold a press conference.
- Participate in seminars.
- Create your own special newsletter.
- Create outdoor advertising.

After the exhibition

Objective:

- To develop positive relations with customers/potential customers.
- To get new business.

Actions:

- Continue advertising campaign.
- Carry out direct mail/e-mailshots to customers/potential customers who visited exhibition stand.
- Sales personnel to make follow-up personal visits to most promising of these customers/potential customers.

The most important of all the things that I have listed pre-exhibition is to get the key information about your company and the products you are exhibiting into the exhibition catalogue, and particularly into the electronic version of the catalogue and onto the exhibition website. Most visitors to major exhibitions are in a hurry and don't want to waste time just wandering round. Many will not even get the exhibition catalogue. Instead they will initially plan their visit by looking at the information on the exhibition website and selecting the companies and products that they are interested in. When they arrive at the exhibition venue they will go to a visitor service desk, input this information and be given an itinerary that allows them to visit all of the stands they want in the most time-effective way.

Examples of strategies involving exhibitions

Examples of strategies and tactics involving exhibitions are shown below:

Strategy – increase exhibition coverage

Tactics:

- Increase attendance and stand size at major industry exhibitions.
- Use government assistance for overseas exhibitions.
- Encourage overseas distributors to exhibit more and supply equipment and personnel as support.

Strategy – introduce new product

Tactics:

- Carry out high-key product launch.
- Support product launch with advertising campaign.
- Support product launch by exhibiting at major exhibitions.

Summary

- Selling requires good sales-support tools. The key tools used by most companies are sales literature, presentations and exhibitions.
- The cost of printing brochures and data sheets is a major expense for many companies. There is a trend towards keeping pdf files of the material on the company website and encouraging customers to download the material they need and print it off themselves.

- Presentations make very effective sales tools and are also useful for training your sales team.
- Exhibitions can be a good showcase for a company's products, but they are expensive and the reasons for being at a major exhibition must be carefully considered beforehand and the cost justified. The size of an exhibition stand matters, both in terms of a company being able to properly exhibit its products and also in terms of the impression that the stand will make on customers and potential customers.
- Exhibition participation must be supported by a media plan, the details of which will vary depending on the message that a company wants to get across and the budget that it has available. This plan must also include follow-up of potential customers after the exhibition.

Chapter nine
Products and pricing

Companies have to be flexible if they want to succeed. They have to be prepared to modify or replace products as the marketplace and their customers' requirements change. A company manufacturing audio-cassette players in the 1980s would have had to change to portable CD players in the 1990s and to iPods in the last 10 years. Video recorders were replaced by DVD recorders and now these are being replaced by Blu-Ray and hard-disk recorders or by downloading films from the internet. Each of these products satisfied the same basic customer need, but at a different moment in time. If the companies had not changed products, they would have gone out of business.

These are major changes where generations of products have been superseded by new ones, but with many products there is a gradual change as new features are added and new versions are developed. This is particularly true with consumer goods that are manufactured in large quantities. Six months is a long time in the development of mobile phones or laptop computers. New products come out with new functionality or new features, and within months other manufacturers bring out their own products with the same features or functionality. It is a similar picture with fast-moving consumer goods like breakfast cereals and chocolate bars, except that here instead of features or functionality the variations are usually in size or flavours and the new products are marketed in parallel to the originals. A good example of this is Nestlé's Kit Kat chocolate bar. The UK's largest selling chocolate bar started as a four-finger bar in milk chocolate, but is now available in two-finger, four-finger and a one-finger 'Chunky' range, with variants of some of these available in plain chocolate, dark chocolate, white chocolate, orange chocolate, mint chocolate or with a layer of peanut butter!

With industrial goods and services the situation is somewhat different. The purchaser of a mobile phone or laptop computer will probably replace it after a few years, because it will be out of date, will lack functionality or may even have stopped working. Industrial goods and machines will often remain in operation for 10 years or even more. Manufacturers of these kinds of product need to be very careful how they handle product enhancement or replacement. A customer with several hundred machines of a particular type in his factories would not be happy if the supplier stopped manufacturing that model and replaced it with a new range of machines of a different size with different maintenance and spare-part requirements – even if the new machine had additional functions that offered the customer enhanced benefits.

In service industries new products can be added to a company's product offering, but replacing car windscreens is still replacing car windscreens and repairing IT equipment is still just that.

In order to bring out different ranges of products, variations of products, and products with new features and functions, large manufacturing companies have large R&D and development departments and large marketing organizations. Even for smaller companies, the cost of developing new products or modifying existing ones can be high, both in terms of developing the product itself and in terms of the marketing costs of launching it. So before deciding to develop a new product, all companies need to examine their existing product portfolio and decide which items are nearing the end of their life and which of these can be enhanced to give them a further lease of life. All companies need to manage their product portfolio.

The product portfolio

The growth and decline of all products follows a product life-cycle curve.

Ideally your company will have a portfolio of products, all at different stages in their life cycle, so that balanced growth can be achieved and risks minimized. The concepts of the product life-cycle curve and the product portfolio were explained in Chapter 1.

As an example in this chapter we will consider the products of The Pure Fruit Jam Company, whose product portfolio is shown in Figure 9.1.

FIGURE 9.1   Product portfolio for The Pure Fruit Jam Company

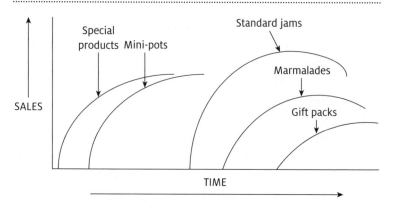

'Special products' and 'mini-pots' are both at the rapid-growth section of their life cycles. 'Standard jams' and 'marmalades' are at the mature stage and 'gift packs' may be heading towards the 'saturation stage'. But the true position of The Pure Fruit Jam Company is more complex, because of the anticipated growth in export business, which means that some products – like 'standard jams', which are at the mature stage of their life cycle in the UK – will get a new lease of life in their overseas sales. The same is true to a lesser extent with 'marmalades' and 'gift packs'.

Relative market growth rate and share

In any market the price levels of the major players tend to be broadly similar. In a stable market the price levels of the major players will gradually move together. This does not mean that all these companies will make the same level of profit. If one company has a very large market share, it will benefit from economies of scale and will have lower costs. The company with the highest market share is likely to have the highest profit margin. It is therefore more able to withstand a price war. Its market share also indicates its ability to generate cash. Market share is therefore very important and it should be your aim to achieve market dominance wherever possible.

Cash flow is the most important factor in considering your product portfolio, and your company's ability to generate cash will be dependent, to a large extent, on the degree of market dominance that you have over your competitors.

Some years ago the Boston Consulting Group developed a matrix for classifying a portfolio of products based on relative market shares and relative market growth rates. The 'Boston matrix' is now widely used by companies to consider their product portfolio.

The products are colourfully described as:

- STARS: high market share/high market growth (cash neutral).
- CASH COWS: high market share/low market growth (cash generation).
- QUESTION MARKS: low market share/high market growth (cash drain).
- DOGS: low market share/low market growth (cash neutral).

Relative market share is the ratio of your market share to the market share of your biggest competitor. It indicates the level of market dominance that you have over your competitors.

Market growth rate is important for two reasons. In a fast-growing market the sales of a product can grow more quickly than in a slow-growing or stable one. In increasing sales, the product will absorb a high level of cash to support increasing advertising, sales coverage, sales support and possibly even investment in additional plant and machinery. High market growth is normally taken as 10 per cent per annum or more.

The products are entered into the quadrants of the matrix as shown in Figure 9.2:

FIGURE 9.2   Ideal product development sequence

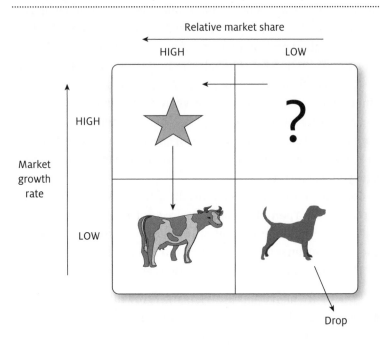

- Question marks can be either newly launched products that have not yet fulfilled expectation, or products that are declining and need further evaluation as to their long-term viability.
- Dogs have low market share and are generally unprofitable. These products would be considered as those that could be dropped from the product portfolio.
- Stars have a high cost in spending on marketing and research and development, but also contribute considerably to profits. They are broadly speaking neutral from the point of view of cash generation.
- Cash cows are mature products with a high market share but low market growth. They generate high profits and require only a small amount of marketing investment and no research and development spending to keep them where they are.

Example

Figure 9.3 shows the current position of the product portfolio of The Pure Fruit Jam Company.

FIGURE 9.3 Portfolio matrix for The Pure Fruit Jam Company

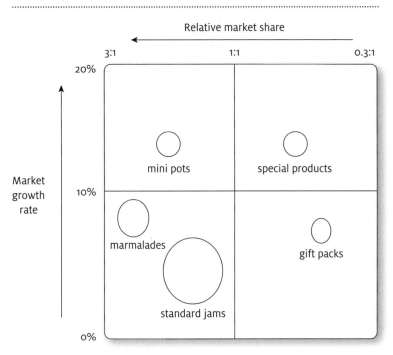

The Pure Fruit Jam Company is very ambitious with its export plans. It wants to move 'standard jams' and 'marmalades' from their current positions as cash cows, towards the area of being stars. 'Mini-pots' are already stars. It wants to move 'special products' from being a question mark to become a star and to revive the fortunes of 'gift packs' from being a dog to become a question mark again.

Product strategies generally involve adding new products, dropping or rationalizing products or modifying your existing products in some way. Modifications can involve increasing performance or adding additional features. This does not necessarily just relate to the requirements of your existing markets. If you have decided to move into exporting your products or if you already have an established export business and want to expand into new geographical areas, you may find that you need to modify your product or develop different versions or different products for different markets.

An example of this is with regard to regulations for machinery and particularly for equipment destined for particular industries, which can be as diverse as the chemical industry or food industry. For the food industry in particular, there are often different regulations for certain kinds of equipment for use in Europe, the United States and Japan.

Some estimates suggest that countries outside Europe and North America will account for up to 80 per cent of global growth between the years 2000 and 2050, so the product requirements of emerging markets will become increasingly important. This will include specific products such as mobile phones and laptops that can be recharged by solar power and water pumps that can be turned by hand. But it will also include more mundane requirements that specific local conditions dictate. An example of this is the refrigerator. Any manufacturer of fridges will know that most US fridges are much larger than those used in Europe. So most multinational fridge manufacturers will have one range for the United States and another for Europe. But Panasonic looked at local conditions around Asia and realized that it also needed a separate version for the Indonesian market with big compartments to store lots of two litre bottles. Indonesians boil water to purify it in the morning and then put it in the fridge to cool. But they need less space for vegetables, because they tend to buy them fresh and use them on the same day.

Examples of product strategies

The following are the main types of strategy that you can adopt for your products with examples of the tactics that could be used to support them.

Strategy – change product portfolio/mix

Tactics:

- Offer only one product line.
- Expand your product line to cover a wider market.
- Develop separate products for different markets.
- Make different versions of the product with different names for different markets.
- Acquire new products that complement existing ones through the acquisition of new companies.

Strategy – drop, add or modify products

Tactics:

- Drop marginal products.
- Develop new products to supersede old ones.
- Launch modified product.

Strategy – change design, quality or performance

Tactics:

- Establish a quality image through the development of quality products.
- Distinguish your product from those of your competitors in the eyes of your customers.
- Establish a reputation for innovation.
- Create new uses for your existing product by improving performance or by adding exclusive features.

Strategy – consolidate/standardize the product

Tactics:

- Rationalize your product line.
- Drop expensive extras/specials.

Product pricing

Pricing is a key factor in marketing strategy. It can be a major determinant of whether your marketing objectives will be achieved. Its role needs to be established in relation to your product portfolio, the life cycles of your products and the objectives that you have for sales turnover and market share.

It is generally true to say that the price level of a product will determine the demand for that product. The price that you sell your product at and the quantity you sell will determine the profit you will make from these sales.

If you reduce your price you would expect to increase the demand for your product. We showed the theory of this in Chapter 1. From an accounting point of view it makes no sense to ever sell a product at a loss. From a marketing perspective, however, you often have to consider the 'chicken and egg' situation. If the product is too highly priced, it may never sell in the quantities necessary for economies of scale to allow the product to be produced profitably. Many large companies with good financial backing have seen this and have been prepared to initially sell products at the market price, rather than a price based upon initial cost. This has enabled them to build up market share quickly and then to make profits. Pricing must ultimately be related to costs, but cost is not the only factor that must be used to determine price in the marketing environment.

Types of pricing strategy

There are many types of pricing strategies and tactics that can be considered. Most can, however, be broadly classified as either skimming policies or penetration policies.

● *Skimming*: this involves entering the market at a high price level and 'skimming' off as much profit as possible. As competition enters the market, the price level would be adjusted as necessary. This type of strategy can only be adopted by a company that has a clear lead over the competition. A company with a product that is way ahead of those of its competitors can successfully adopt a skimming policy. The problem with a skimming policy is that the high profits generated do encourage competitors to enter the market. A good example of this is Apple with the iPad. Apple sold 4 million iPads in the first six months after its launch, but the price was so high that it encouraged competitors to bring out cheaper copies. Apple had a strategy to combat this, and rather than move the price level of the original iPad down drastically they brought out a 'mini' version of the iPad at a much lower price.

● *Penetration*: this is the opposite of skimming. With this type of strategy a company sets the price deliberately low. A penetration policy encourages more customers to purchase the product, which increases the company's sales turnover and also its market share. This in turn means that the company will be able to benefit from economies of scale in manufacture at an earlier stage than would otherwise be possible. A company operating a penetration policy may be initially selling at a loss on the basis that the price will rapidly achieve a level of turnover where the product becomes profitable.

Premium pricing

Some products sell at a high price, because of what they are or because of the reputation of the company that makes them. Examples of this are designer goods and quality sports cars like Porsche or Ferrari. The concept of a quality product selling at a quality price is an important one. A price that is too low can be just as much of a disincentive to sales as a price that is too high.

Price leadership

The market leader is in a unique position. It is likely that other companies will set their prices on the basis of the leader's price and will move prices after it moves – whether up or down. Because of its high market share, the market leader is in a strong position to react to price changes from smaller competitors.

The life-cycle effect

The position of a product on its life-cycle curve or in a particular quadrant of the Boston matrix will also determine the type of pricing strategy that is relevant. If a product is at the saturation stage of its life cycle and is also a 'cash cow' with a high and established market share, it would be illogical to consider price cutting to try to increase market share. It would be far better to keep the price high for as long as possible so as to milk the product and provide profits to support newer products. If, on the other hand, a product is at an early stage of its life cycle and is a 'question mark', it may well make sense to consider a penetration policy to increase market share.

Discounting

Pricing policy does not just relate to list prices. Discounting strategies are an integral part of the price equation. They are mainly relevant if you are selling through distribution channels, although even if you are selling directly to end-users, quantity discounts can be used. Discounts can be used to encourage larger individual orders or can be based upon the total amount of business placed in a given period of time. They can be used to encourage customers to buy from your company alone and not to spread the business between you and your competitors.

A company with a portfolio of products has an advantage over a single-product company in terms of its pricing policies. It can gear the pricing strategies for particular products to the position of those products in their life cycles and the overall requirements of the company for profit. It can decide to forego profit today on certain products in order to increase market share, and to take its profits on other products that are more established in the marketplace. With a portfolio of products it is possible to have a true pricing plan rather than just a collection of individual pricing strategies.

Examples of pricing strategies

The following are some of the main types of strategy that you can adopt for pricing with examples of the tactics that could be used to support them.

Strategy – change price, terms or conditions for particular product groups in particular market segments

Tactics:

- Set price at 10 per cent below market leader.
- Devise strategy to meet specific pricing policies of competitors.
- Reduce price of product to maximize sales (to allow increased production and reduce unit production cost).
- Price product low and obtain maximum profit on spare parts.
- Price product high and use low mark-up on spare parts.

Strategy – skimming policy

Tactics:

- Set price of new product at a level 30 per cent above previous products.
- Sell on new revolutionary design features and benefits.
- Be prepared to reduce price as volume increases if competitors enter market.

Strategy – penetration policy

Tactics:

- Set low price for new product to discourage competitors from entering market.
- Increase turnover to level where product becomes profitable at this price level.

Strategy – discount policies

Tactics:

- Offer quantity discount to encourage larger unit purchases.
- Offer discount to encourage online purchasing.
- Offer retrospective discount based on level of purchases this year.
- Offer discount level for next year based on level of purchases this year.

Launching a new product

When you launch a new product it can either be replacing or superseding an existing one or it may be a completely new product of a type that you have never offered before. Even if the product is completely new to your company, there will still be information available about competing products and the market for them. If the new product is superseding an existing product, then you will have information relating to the sales of that product and its markets.

There can be many reasons for developing or adding a new product, but most are the result of analysing your product portfolio and either deciding that a product needs replacing or identifying a gap in the portfolio that presents you with a potential opportunity. Developing a new product is an expensive and time-consuming process and its launch needs to be carefully planned. Our example is for a new product being launched by The Pure Fruit Jam Company.

Example

The Pure Fruit Jam Company entered the field of flavoured marmalades two years ago and immediately saw growth in the sale of its marmalade products. It initially launched whisky and brandy-flavoured marmalades. It carried out further market research and now intends to launch two new products next year – cointreau-flavoured and rum-flavoured marmalades. It has prepared a marketing plan for the new products and the key information from this is given (pages 191–95).

Sales (History/Budget)

TABLE 9.1   Sales of flavoured marmalades

THE PURE FRUIT JAM COMPANY

SALES FIGURES (Historical and forecast)
SALES AREA: ALL

YEAR (all values in £k)	20X3	20X4	20X5	20X6	20X7	20X8
					←—— Forecast ——→	
WHISKY MARMALADE		15	65	85	110	140
BRANDY MARMALADE		10	52	70	100	130
RUM MARMALADE				20	40	60
COINTREAU MARMALADE				20	40	60
TOTAL	0	25	117	195	290	390

Strategic markets

Quality shops

We have found a ready market for our flavoured marmalades in quality shops and expect the bulk of the product to sell through these.

Hotels

Jarvis and MacDonald Hotels have taken well to mini-pots with our whisky and brandy-flavoured marmalades. We expect them also to take our new flavours.

Marketing objectives

- to grow sales of flavoured marmalades from £117,000 now to £390,000 within three years;
- to grow sales of rum-flavoured marmalade to £60,000 within three years;

- to grow sales of cointreau-flavoured marmalade to £60,000 within three years.

Marketing strategies

Products
Add/modify products:

- Launch rum and cointreau-flavoured marmalade.
- Launch new-look gift packs.

Pricing
Discount policies:

- Offer retrospective discount to major outlets based on level of annual purchases.

Promotion
Change advertising/sales promotion:

- Carry out high-key product launch for rum and cointreau-flavoured marmalades.

Distribution
Add distribution channels:

- Expand outlets in major cities in North and Scotland.
- Sell mini-pots through Hotel Catering Services Ltd.

Expand website:

- To allow online purchases.

The product launch for the new range of breakfast marmalades in the UK will take place in June 20X6 with a press launch on 26 June and a trade launch on 27 June. The products will also be shown at the Foodex exhibition in September 20X6. They will be carrying out a press advertising campaign to support that.

They have prepared an action plan for the product launch and this is shown in Table 9.2.

TABLE 9.2   Action plan for The Pure Fruit Jam Company for its UK product launch

ACTION PLAN – Product launch for specialist marmalades

DEPARTMENT: SALES & MARKETING

Aim	Action	By	Start	Finish	Cost
Carry out product launch	Prepare launch package	JAW	1.1.X6	1.6.X6	£5,000
	Manufacture samples	AKH	1.3.X6	15.5.X6	£3,000
	Book venues and hotels	EBG	1.11.X5	1.1.X6	£8,000
	Book stand design and build	JAW	1.1.X6	1.6.X6	£13,000
	Commission launch video	JAW	1.1.X6	1.6.X6	£10,000
	Book advertising	EBG	1.3.X6	1.4.X6	£15,000
	Send out invitations	EBG	1.3.X6	1.4.X6	£300

The launch package itself consists of a number of individual items:

● press release;
● leaflet;
● launch video;
● letter to key customers;
● letter to distributors;
● press advert;
● jam 'kits' – including a sample of each jam.

The costs of preparing the press release and of preparing and sending out letters and invitations are included in the normal marketing budget. The leaflet will continue to be used for the products after the launch and is therefore included in the overall budget for sales literature.

These costs are not included in the details of product launch expenditure shown in Table 9.3. Similarly the cost of the advertising campaign is included in the company's annual advertising budget rather than being allocated to the product launch itself.

The organizers have booked the conference facilities at the Cumberland Hotel in Knightsbridge for an internal company launch and a press launch on 26 June and for a launch to key customers and a launch to key distributors on 27 June. At the same time they have made a block booking of rooms at the hotel for key customers and distributors. If enough rooms are left over, they will use these for their own staff, but if not they will book additional rooms at a smaller hotel nearby. Before they can send out the invitations they will have to update the list of who should be invited – from the press, from customers and from distributors. Details of their product launch expenditure are given in Table 9.3.

TABLE 9.3 Product launch costs for The Pure Fruit Jam Company for their new marmalade range

PRODUCT LAUNCH COSTS
Name of product: New marmalade range

Location: Cumberland Hotel
Date: 26–27 June 20X6
Agency: Top Notch Advertising

COSTS	£
Hire of hotel room and facilities	3,000
Design, supply and build launch stand	8,000
Artwork, photographic panels	5,000
Launch video	10,000
Sample packs	3,000
Launch dinner	3,000
Hotel bills/expenditure for launch staff	2,000
TOTAL	34,000

As part of the continuing launch programme, The Pure Fruit Jam Company has also taken a stand at the Foodex exhibition at the NEC in Birmingham. Details of the cost involved in this are given in Table 9.4.

TABLE 9.4   Exhibition costs for The Pure Fruit Jam Company

EXHIBITION COSTS

Name of exhibition: Foodex
Location: NEC Birmingham
Date: 6–8 September 20X6
Stand size: 32m² (4m × 8m)
Stand contractor: Top Notch Advertising

COSTS	£
Stand space rental	4,000
Design, supply and build	8,000
Artwork, photographic panels	4,000
Rental of carpets, furniture, lights, phone, etc	2,000
Hotel bills/expenditure for stand staff	2,000
TOTAL	20,000

Summary

- Companies have to be flexible if they want to succeed. They have to be prepared to modify or replace products as the marketplace and their customers' requirements change.
- The growth and decline of all products follows a life-cycle curve, Ideally a company will have a portfolio of products, all at different stages in their life cycle, so that balanced growth can be achieved and risk minimized.
- Cash flow is the most important factor in considering a product portfolio, and a company's ability to generate cash will be largely dependent on the degree of market dominance that it has over its competitors.
- It is often necessary to modify products, or to develop different versions or different products for different markets.

- Product strategies usually involve a company changing its product portfolio by dropping, adding or modifying products.
- The role of pricing needs to be established in relation to a company's product portfolio, the life cycle of its products and its objectives for sales turnover and market share.
- There are many types of pricing strategy, but most can be classified as either skimming or penetration policies.
- There can be many reasons for developing a new product, but most are the result of a company analysing its product portfolio and either deciding that a product needs replacing or identifying a gap in the product portfolio that presents it with a potential opportunity.
- Developing a new product is an expensive and time-consuming process and its launch needs to be carefully planned.

Chapter ten
Application selling

Application selling is a market development technique that has been used widely in recent years. It involves finding a successful application for your product and promoting this in other geographical areas or in other industries. It applies more to industrial products and services than to consumer products. An example might be a company that sells filters. If it has been successful in selling its product into the dairy industry, then it may be able to increase its business by selling the same product into other industries where the same type of filtration is required, such as the wider food industry or the pharmaceutical industry.

Application selling can involve using any of the four 'P's. We will concentrate mainly on 'Promotion' and 'Place', but in some cases 'Product' and 'Price' can also play their part.

Different customers have different needs. They do not all require the same product and they do not all require the same product benefits. Even with an individual product, not all customers will buy it for the same reasons. As we saw in Chapter 3, market segmentation allows you to consider the markets and segments of those markets that you are actually in.

A company selling equipment in corrosion-resistant materials may say that a major market for its equipment is the chemical industry, but in practice its major market may actually be just one sector of the chemical industry that uses large amounts of acids or alkalis such as fertilizer manufacture. A company selling equipment to the food industry may actually only have major sales in the dairy industry.

But just because this particular market segment for your products is quite narrow, this does not mean that you cannot increase your sales by finding the same market segment in other geographical areas or a similar market segment in your existing sales areas.

In Chapter 3 we saw how you can use the Ansoff matrix to consider new marketing strategies. It can be seen from this matrix that the least risky way to try to expand your business is in the areas you know best – that is, with your existing products in your existing markets.

This is where application selling comes in. If you have been successful selling a product in one particular application, it should be possible to get more sales in that particular application.

The concept

First look at your sales in your home market, because this is where you could make progress quickly. But application selling can find you additional business in other areas as well. The main possibilities are:

- finding more customers in sales areas where you are already selling the product(s) into this application;
- finding potential customers in sales areas where you are either selling very little or selling none of the product(s) into this application;
- finding potential customers in sales areas handled by your distributors;
- finding potential customers overseas in areas handled by your distributors;
- understanding more fully your customers' requirements and considering modifications or improvements to your product, or even new products for this application.

Example

A company manufacturing industrial valves decides to look at its home market. It has identified a significant market as being the water industry. It has two applications in this industry. One is control valves on sedimentation tanks and the other is non-return valves for pumping systems. It needs to analyse its sales figures for the last few years to separate out sales of valves sold into this one industry, and to further split the sales by the products sold for the two specific applications. It needs to show these sales by individual sales area.

Table 10.1 shows the result of its analysis for control valves.

TABLE 10.1   Sales for an application by sales area

SALES OF DCV VALVES IN THE WATER INDUSTRY

YEAR:	20X4 (£k)	20X5 (£k)	20X6 (£k)
Area 1	220	222	216
Area 2	120	130	120
Area 3	350	400	430
Area 4	3	2	3
Area 5	0	0	0
Total	693	754	769

The results for non-return valves are similar.

The next step is to look at the sales and distribution arrangements in each area. The company can immediately see that it has its highest levels of sales where it has direct sales using its own sales personnel in Areas 1, 2 and 3, and that it has virtually no sales in Areas 4 and 5, which are handled by external distributors. Further analysis of the sales figures shows that its major sales are split between a number of different types of customer. So it is able to split and analyse the sales by the following customer types:

● sales to end-users;
● sales to engineering companies carrying out new projects;
● sales to equipment manufacturers using valves in their packages.

These three different types of customer have different requirements:

● The end-user wants to replace old or faulty equipment or to improve a system.

- The engineering company want the most cost-effective solution for its control requirement.
- The equipment manufacturer wants to be able to standardize on one piece of equipment in its package – also at a cost-effective price.

So how can you use the type of information gathered in the above example to help you to grow your sales?

In order to carry out application selling, you need to put together a set of tools that can be used to train both your own and your distributors' salesforces to sell your product into an application. Remember and understand that sales personnel are usually too busy making sure that they achieve their sales targets every month to be able or motivated to carry out what I would call market development. Equally, distributors have a range of products to sell, and will concentrate on those that are easiest to sell and guarantee the best return. Don't expect distributors to develop markets for you.

Not only do you need to prepare the training material, but you also need to carry out structured training as part of an action plan for growing sales in the application. For overseas non-English-speaking markets, the material needs to be sent out prior to the training so that it can be translated into the local language. Because of the investment in time and money for this training, it is more cost effective to prepare material for a number of different applications at the same time (probably three to five different applications).

In a larger company the marketing department can carry out the market research, analyse the results and put together a package of sales-support material. An alternative is to make a 'one-off' investment by using an independent marketing consultant to do the work for you. In a smaller company, you may well have to do the work yourself in addition to your normal work!

The package of sales-support material will usually consist of the following:

- *An application manual*: this documents all the key information on the application – the industry, the size of the market, the application itself, the benefits you are selling to the customer, references, application photos as well as details of your main competitors and their competing products. This is usually a Word document containing material that will be used in the presentations.

- *A training presentation*: this is a PowerPoint presentation to be used in training your own salesforce and your distributors. It contains details of the industry market, the applications, the benefits to the customer, references, application photos and details of your main competitors, together with a SWOT analysis of your competitors for the product used in the application.
- *A customer presentation*: this is also a PowerPoint presentation and is used by your salesforce and your distributors' salesforces to make presentations to customers. It contains most of the material from the training presentation, except for the competition material, and in addition it contains key information and benefits for the products you are proposing.
- In some cases additional sales leaflets, data sheets or flyers may also be required.

This may sound like a lot of material to prepare, but bear in mind that much of the material is common to the different documents. Since you will use a common format, it will be used to prepare documents for more than one application. Also, because the documents are prepared electronically, they do not need to be printed off or used as hard copies. Since the documents are available electronically, your overseas distributors can quickly produce versions in their own languages, both for training and presentation purposes.

But let's start at the beginning. The first thing you need to do is to decide what applications you have that have the potential to grow. Although you can carry out the process for one application, it is more cost effective if you do it for several at the same time. You can then decide whether it will be more effective to pass the applications to your sales organization and distribution network in one go or as a drip feed of (say) one application every six months. It is probably wise to limit the number of applications to a maximum of about five or you will risk spreading the sales effort too thinly.

The next thing that you need to do is to select your applications. The best way to do this is to carry out some initial analysis of figures for your sales by industry and then to consult your sales team about what they consider to be key applications. Remember that you are looking for applications where you can grow the business. If you are looking to grow extra business in your overseas markets, the applications could be some of your most successful applications that have a high level of sales in your home market. In your home market these applications will already be well known to your sales personnel and distributors, so for growth here you will be looking for an application that a particular salesperson or distributor has pioneered, and that is successful in one or two sales areas but has not yet been spread into your other sales areas.

Information on sales by application should be available in your sales data, although it may need some expert interpretation to make sure that it is interpreted properly. Also individual sales people or sales managers may say that they have a specific application that they think could have greater potential. To prepare a list you need to consult widely with your key sales and marketing personnel. Ideally, you need to get these key sales and marketing personnel together. But since it is costly to take salespeople off the road, I find one of the most cost- and time-effective ways of doing this is to have the meeting by 'web conference'. In this way you can talk to people in other offices or working from home. A 'web conference' uses a facility available from a number of companies that specialize in this method of communication. All the people taking part are given website details and a password. They can then log on to the website shortly before the web conference is scheduled. At the same time they call a conference-call phone number that has been provided. All of the people who have logged on to the web conference can talk on the conference call and they all see the same information on their PC. So you can show sales data on Excel spreadsheets or in PowerPoint presentations and discussion can take place on the telephone conference call. Other participants can e-mail material for discussion to you prior to the web conference taking place, so that this material can also be shown.

Objectives

The purpose of application selling is to increase your level of sales. So once you have your list of applications you need to decide what is possible. For example:

- *Objective*: To grow sales in the chemical industry by £200,000 per year for each of the next three years.
- *Strategy*: Target our five top applications in the chemical industry and develop a plan to promote application selling.

Preparation of key material

Once you have your list and it has been trimmed down to no more than five applications, there are a number of key steps to be followed to prepare the material that you need for each of them:

- Obtain information relating to the market size for the industry.
- Analyse your own sales by area, region, etc.
- Put together a list of your actual applications in this industry or industry sector.
- Where applicable, put together a simple flow diagram for the process where your product is being used.
- Put together a reference list of customers using your product in this application.
- Use your salesforce to obtain site photographs of your equipment installed. (For this you need to get the customers' permission; if you have good contacts, they may even take the photographs for you.)
- Collect information from competitors' websites of products they manufacture that compete with yours. From this, prepare SWOT analyses of how you and your product compare with them and theirs.
- List the key benefits that you offer the customer.

Several of these steps will require input from key sales personnel and so further 'web conferences' may be required.

In going through each stage of the preparation of key material, I think it would be useful to give worked examples. For this I will use The Gear Pump Company. Its pumps are used for transferring liquids in a wide range of industries, including the chemical, oil, water and food industries. In the chemical industry it has a number of application segments including adhesives, soaps and detergents, plastic and resin manufacture, and paints and pigments. As one of the successful applications that it wants to promote, it has chosen 'paints and paint pigments' (see the discussion below of this example).

The market

It is useful for your salespeople to know how large the market that you are looking at is. By that I mean the total market. Is it a £100 million or a £10 million turnover industry? In some cases you may even be able to define the market for your product, if each application is for a particular type of site and you know how much or how many of your product could be sold on that site. An example is in the supply of equipment for use in water treatment plants, pulp and paper mills, coal mines or power stations. For all of these industries, information is published in many countries giving the number of sites and often their size. So a company supplying equipment for use in sewage treatment plants in the UK would know that the number of plants is several thousand, but that only a few hundred are large enough to require large treatment equipment. Equally there are only a few dozen pulp or paper mills, power stations or coal mines. But for many industries the information given is not so exact.

Information about overall market size for most major industries is available on the internet. An initial search can be carried out by making a simple search on Google. So if you want information on fruit juice production, just type in 'fruit juice production'. This will get you websites with data on how to produce fruit juice as well as websites giving statistical data. So you need to refine your search. Perhaps try 'fruit juice production statistics'. Similarly, if you are really only interested in fruit juice production in Europe or just the UK, type in 'fruit juice production + Europe' or 'fruit juice production + UK'.

Example

The Gear Pump Company is looking for information on the paint industry. Its planners are only looking for general information to include in a short summary at the start of its paint industry manual. They try various searches, including 'world paint market', 'paint production', 'paint market + statistics' and 'European paint market + turnover'. They find lots of market research companies offering to sell market reports on various aspects of the paint industry. But they also find a number of useful sites, including the National Paint & Coatings Association (NPCA – **www.paint.org**) and The European Council of producers and importers of paints, printing inks and artists' colours (CEPE – **www.cepe.org**), that provide free information. From the CEPE website they find links to all the trade associations for paint in the EU. The NPCA site gives worldwide data and US data and also includes statistics on worldwide sales of different categories of paints into different industries. The sites of CEPE and the trade association websites give much more detailed data for the UK/EU. They also find a free report entitled *The World Market for Paint 2003*. All of this information has been obtained in less than an hour and at no cost to the company. From this they are able to produce the summary shown in Table 10.2.

TABLE 10.2   Summary of worldwide paint market

Paint industry – key facts
- The worldwide paint market has a turnover of about $60 billion.
- Sales have increased by 20 per cent since 1995.
- Paint is now an international business.
- Household paint accounts for 57 per cent of the market.
- Industrial coatings account for 30 per cent of the market. These are sold mainly into the automotive, furniture, electronic equipment, aerospace and shipping industries.
- There is heavy investment in both R&D and new capital equipment.

This summary is placed in the application manual and also in the training presentation. (It does not go into the customer presentation – the customers probably already know their market!)

Sales analysis

For this, you need to analyse your sales figures for the last few years and separate out sales of your product sold into this one industry and to further split the sales by the products sold for the specific application. You need to show these sales by individual sales area.

Example

The figures for The Gear Pump Company are shown in Table 10.3.

TABLE 10.3   Sales for an application by sales area

SALES OF GPI GEAR PUMPS IN THE PAINT INDUSTRY

YEAR:	20X4 (£k)	20X5 (£k)	20X6 (£k)
South	276	282	246
Midlands	143	127	185
North	424	573	622
Wales	5	12	7
Scotland/NI	0	0	0
Total	848	994	1,060

From this they can see that their sales are high in the South of England, the Midlands and the North, where they have their own sales teams, but are virtually non-existent in Wales, Scotland and Northern Ireland, where they rely on distributors.

Actual applications

You need to define the actual applications that you have in the industry. This helps your sales team to target the applications and make potential customers aware that you can satisfy their requirements. Some of your sales team may already have this information, but if not finding it may involve some site visits or discussions with existing customers. If you supply linkage systems for the agricultural industry, it is important that your sales team understand that these systems are only supplied to tractor manufacturers, and only up to 'size 3' if that is the industry standard for denoting tractor size.

Example

The Gear Pump Company already has information on its computer showing the products being pumped. From this it is able to conclude that the products that its devices can pump in the paint industry are:

- water-soluble paints;
- oil-based paints;
- latex-based paints;
- paint pigments;
- solvents and dispersants.

From discussion with the sales team and key existing customers, the company can list the actual applications as:

- general transfer duties;
- paint mixing;
- filling lines;
- filling and emptying tanks.

From the analysis the company can also confirm which duties require special materials and those for which it can use standard materials. This information is included in the application manual and also in the training and customer presentations.

The sales team is also able to prepare a list of typical specifications for pumps used in each of these applications. It includes details of pump sizes and materials of construction. This is shown in Table 10.4.

Flow diagrams and location diagrams

For many products this will not be applicable, but if you supply components that are used in an industry such as food manufacturing or car manufacturing, where there is a clear process, then it is useful to be able to show in a simple diagram, roughly where the component would be located.

TABLE 10.4 Typical specifications for internal gear pumps for use in the paint industry

TYPICAL SPECIFICATIONS FOR INTERNAL GEAR PUMPS IN THE PAINT INDUSTRY

Process	Item no	Medium	Typical pump size	Typical pump materials	Approvals/ certification	Comments
Bulk transfer	1	paint	GPl2/GPl3	aluminium		
Bulk transfer	1	solvent	GPl2/GPl3	stainless steel	ATEX	
Bulk transfer	1	paint pigments	GPl2/GPl3	cast iron		
Bulk transfer	1	dispersant	GPl2/GPl3	stainless steel		
Paint mixing	2,3,4 +5	paint	GPl1	aluminium		
Pumping to filling machines	6 + 7	paint	GPl2/GPl3	aluminium		Use of pulsation dampener recommended

Features and benefits

Although your customers purchase products, what they are really purchasing is a solution to their requirements. There has to be a reason for them to purchase from you rather than from your competitors and this has to be the benefits that they get from the key features of your product. In many cases a 'feature' will mean nothing to your customers unless you explain to them the 'benefit' that feature gives them. You need to list the key features of your product and the benefits that they give. This will be a key slide in your customer presentation.

Example

The Gear Pump Company has listed out the following features and benefits for their products for the paint industry in Table 10.5.

TABLE 10.5 An example of 'features' and 'benefits'

Features	Benefits
Compact size	Low space requirement for pump and for *in situ* maintenance
Wide range of material options	Reduced risk of corrosion means lower maintenance costs
Hardened components	Less wear and reduced maintenance costs
We have ATEX certification	Our pumps can be used in explosive environments

Reference list

To gain credibility for your product in the application, you need to be able to show your salespeople, your distributors and your potential customers that you have a track record. One of the best ways of achieving this is to provide a list of references. But be careful! Make sure that you check out all of the references and make sure that your equipment is still there and that the customer is happy with it. Make

TABLE 10.6 Example of a reference list

SELECTED REFERENCES IN THE PAINT INDUSTRY

Segment	User/ customer	Process	Medium	Pump type	Comments
Paint	PI Paints	filling machines	household paint	GPI2	Al with pulsation dampener
Paint	Quickspray	bulk transfer	oil-based paint	GPI3	Al
Paint	B & X	transfer to mixing vessel	varnish	GPI2	SS
Paint	PI Paints	transfer to mixing vessel	latex-based paint	GPI3	Al
Paint	PI Pigments	transfer to mixing vessel	pigment	GPI1	CA
Paint	Dilu Paints	bulk transfer	water-soluble paints	GPI3	Al
Paint	Dilu Paints	filling machines	paint containing solvents	GPI2	SS with pulsation dampener

sure that you can include some references from important users in the industry and keep the list short – no more than 5 to 10 references.

Example

The Gear Pump Company makes a list of actual installations from its database and then discusses these with the sales team. Some are removed from the list, because the factory has closed, pumps have been replaced or there is some problem. The remaining list is whittled down to a final list of seven applications with five reference customers, including the two best customers in the paint industry – PI Paints and Dilu Paints. The list is shown in Table 10.6.

Photographs

Just as with reference lists, photographs of a product *in situ* provide further evidence to potential clients that you have a track record. This is also important with the sales teams of your distributors, who also need convincing that it is worth the effort of trying to sell your product into this new (to them) application area. For presentations, the resolution of the photographs does not need to be as high as for photographs used in brochures or exhibition panels, so photos taken on a normal digital camera by your sales team will be perfectly adequate. In fact if you were to use only high-resolution photos, you would find that the file size of your presentations quickly exceeds 20 gigabytes and that they cannot easily be e-mailed. Photography is a sensitive issue and many companies do not allow photography on their sites and do not want suppliers to use photographs taken on their sites, just in case they show information that could be of use to competitors. So if you think that site photographs would enhance your presentations, I would suggest that first of all you search the photo archive in your marketing department. It may have some suitable photographs and customers may already have given permission for these photos to be used for publicity purposes. If this does not yield sufficient material, ask your sales team and your key distributors if they can provide anything. Finally ask key salespeople to approach some key customers who have your equipment installed and ask for permission to take site photographs. You may find they are more willing to allow photography if you limit the use to presentations, or even in some cases just to your own training presentations. You will probably need to submit prints of the final photographs in order to get written approval from the customers.

In your presentation, use a simple caption with each photograph. This should include details of the application and the type/size of product shown. You may decide to include the name of the customer or not – bear in mind that you are just as likely to be showing your presentation to companies that are competitors of your existing customers.

Competitor information

Although you will probably already have a wealth of competitor information in-house, the best way to obtain the most up-to-date information available is to use the internet and go onto their websites. Here you can obtain information about the company, whether it belongs to a larger group, details of its distribution arrangements and an up-to-date list of its products. In many cases there will also be product brochures and data sheets on the website that you can download. All of this material will be up to date, which may not be the case with sales literature that you obtained from an exhibition three years ago.

You are not getting this competitor information to pass on to your customers. It is to help you understand how the company and its products compare with yours and for use in your training presentations. Once you have the competitor material, you need to produce two things for your training presentations:

- a list of the pros and cons of competing products;
- SWOT analyses of your main competitors.

If you prepare a list of the pros and cons of competing products, you will better understand the strengths and weaknesses of your competitor's products and also of your own offerings.

The Gear Pump Company has prepared a list of pros and cons of the product of one of its main competitors in the paint industry – The Lobe Pump Company. This is shown in Table 10.7.

TABLE 10.7   List of pros and cons of a competing product

Pros and cons of Rotary Lobe Pumps

Pros	Cons
Pumphead components in stainless steel	Limited suction lift capability
Compact design	Complicated maintenance
Pressures up to 20 bar	Pulsing flow
Flow rates up to 106 m³/hr	Limited dry running (only with seal flush)
Horizontal or vertical connections	
Fully draining in horizontal configuration	

In Chapter 3 we showed how SWOT analysis can be used to look at your competitors' strengths and weaknesses and how these translate into opportunities for you and into threats to you.

Example

Table 10.8 shows a SWOT analysis that The Gear Pump Company has prepared for its major competitor the Lobe Pump Company.

Additional slides about your main competitors can be prepared using brochures, data sheets, photos and diagrams downloaded from their websites. But make sure that you only do this for the main competitors for this application, otherwise you will confuse your salesforce and distributors.

Preparing the application manual, customer and training presentations

Once you have all the material together, you can complete the application manual, customer presentation and your training presentation.

TABLE 10.8   SWOT analysis for a competitor

Their strengths	Their weaknesses
Wide-ranging distribution	Complicated maintenance
Wide range of products and accessories	Two shafts to seal
Strong brand, good quality	Inexperienced own salesforce
Short lead times	They lack service support

Opportunities for us	Threats to us
We have hardened materials	New product under development
Our relief valves are interchangeable	Their new factory in China
We have ATEX certification	Their new stocking concept
Our new chemical industry salesforce	
They have a high-cost factory in Germany	

The application manual will include all of the key information to be used in both the customer and training presentations:

- an introduction to the industry;
- summary details of the applications that you cover in the industry;
- flow diagrams of the processes (where applicable);
- typical specifications of your product;
- features and benefits of your product;
- details of key competitors for this industry;
- comparison with the features and benefits of the competitors' products;
- general information on your main competitors, including details of their main products;
- SWOT analyses of your main competitors;
- a selected list of references in the industry;
- product and/or site photographs (where applicable).

The customer presentation will include the following:

- an introduction slide;
- summary details of the applications that you cover in the industry;
- flow diagrams of the processes (where applicable);
- typical specifications of your product;
- features and benefits of your product;
- a technical presentation of your product (where applicable), which could be a separate presentation that you may already have;
- a selected list of references in the industry;
- product and/or site photographs (where applicable).

The training presentation will include the following:

- an introduction slide;
- key facts about the industry you are targeting;
- summary details of the applications that you cover in the industry;
- flow diagrams of the processes (where applicable);
- typical specifications of your product;
- features and benefits of your product;
- comparison with the features and benefits of competitors' products;
- general information on your main competitors including details of their main products;
- SWOT analyses of your main competitors;
- a selected list of references in the industry;
- product and/or site photographs (where applicable).

Much of this material is common to both presentations, but the key facts about the industry that is being targeted and all of the information about the competition are only included in the training programme.

The introduction programme

Once you have all of the documentation, you need to implement your introduction plan. This will involve rolling out the project to your sales team. This is best done at a special sales meeting. You also need to roll the project out to your distributors and to your key overseas distributors. The material needs to be sent out to distributors in overseas non-English-speaking markets prior to the training so that it can be translated into the local language. It is also useful if you or your distributors can do some work ahead of the launch to establish the size of the market in their area/country and the key potential customers.

Table 10.9 shows the master plan prepared by The Gear Pump Company for the project. It covers the individual action plans for the collection of material, preparation of presentations and the plans for launching the application project to the sales team, the UK distributors and to key overseas distributors.

TABLE 10.9 Master schedule for application selling project

MASTER SCHEDULE

Area: Application project – 'paint'
Year: 20X6

Month	1 2 3 4 5 6 7 8 9 10 11 12	Responsibility	
Action plan		Dept	Person
Collect information	⟶	Marketing	AJK/EGM
Prepare presentations	⟶	Marketing	BJC
Sales team launch	⟶	Sales	EGM
UK distributor launch	⟶	Sales	EGM
Overseas launches	⟶	Sales	FJK

Controls and update procedures

The purpose of your project is to grow your business by a specific amount. So you need to have feedback and compare your actual results to your forecast (or budgeted) results. This should be done with a quarterly or six-monthly reporting procedure.

Summary

- Application selling is a technique that helps you to grow your business by taking successful applications and promoting them in other geographical areas or in other applications.
- You can find more customers in sales areas where you are already selling your product.
- You can find potential customers in sales areas where you are selling very little.
- You can find potential customers in sales areas handled by your distributors.
- Application selling also helps you to understand more fully your customers' requirements and to consider product modifications, improvements or even the development of new products.
- Since the purpose of application selling is to increase your level of sales, you need to set specific growth objectives and select the strategies that will enable you to achieve them.
- In order to carry out application selling, you need to put together a set of tools that can be used to train both your own salesforce and your distributors' salesforces.
- The package of sales-support material will usually consist of an application manual, a training presentation and a customer presentation.
- Once you have prepared the documentation, you need to launch the application project with structured training to your sales team and your distributors.
- For overseas non-English-speaking markets, the material needs to be sent out prior to the training so that it can be translated into the local language.

Chapter eleven
Getting into overseas markets

If you are confident that you have good products and have a steady level of business in your home markets, perhaps now is the time to look at selling abroad. Selling your existing products into new (export) markets is a medium-risk strategy. It is more risky than trying to expand sales of your existing products in your current markets, but while the risks are greater, the rewards can also be greater. Although expanding your sales abroad gives you major opportunities for growth you need to be aware that the associated costs are higher than selling locally – so margins will usually be lower. Exporting is not without its risks. Language and cultural differences, political instability, currency and payment problems can all pose risks to inexperienced exporters. These are reasons why your export sales should always supplement your local or home sales and not replace them.

The benefits of exporting

Exporting can help you to increase your potential market, increase your turnover, improve your business's reputation, avoid your being over-dependent on your UK sales and provide a buffer to any cyclical deterioration in the UK economy.

According to UK Trade & Investment (UKTI – **www.ukti.gov.uk**) companies that export:

- improve their productivity;
- achieve levels of growth not possible domestically;
- increase the resilience of their revenues and profits;
- achieve economies of scale not possible domestically;
- increase the commercial lifespan of their products and services;
- increase the returns on their investment in R&D;
- improve their financial performance;
- feel the benefit.

Academic research confirms that exporting companies are more productive than non-exporters, achieve stronger financial perform-ance and are more likely to stay in business.

A study of UK companies by Harris and Cher Li showed that firms beginning to export gained a 34 per cent productivity uplift and that those that exported were 11.4 per cent more likely to survive.

Recent surveys by UKTI show that doing business overseas gives companies increased exposure to new ideas. This gives them the opportunity to develop new and improved products and services that can help them to gain and retain competitive advantage at home as well as overseas.

Dabbling in export

Nowadays, any company with an e-commerce website can generate some overseas sales. As long as you have a product to ship (and not a service), you have no limits to your business area. If your company is well promoted and your website attracts attention from search engines, there is no reason why your company cannot pick up some business from anywhere in the world. A customer in France or Australia can buy from you online just as easily as a customer in London or Newcastle. But you need to be careful. Even on your website, you cannot handle overseas business in exactly the same way as you handle your home sales. The goods need to be safely delivered and you need to get paid. Unless you make sure that you get payment by credit card online, getting payment could be difficult. Shipping costs to overseas destinations will be higher than shipping costs to customers in your home market and it may be difficult to make sure that these costs are fully covered. There may be import restrictions in the country you are shipping to. You can easily ship books to Europe or the United States, if you make a proper customs declaration on the package, but sending the same book to certain countries in the Middle East or Far East could result in them being confiscated or returned. I remember once having sales literature returned from India, because the recipient did not want to pay the import duty!

Fortunately most e-commerce website packages include facilities to make taking orders from overseas easier. As well as accepting credit card payment, most packages include the facility for you to take payment via PayPal or WorldPay or even by electronic funds transfer (EFT). With regard to postage and packing, most e-commerce packages allow you to set up special rates that users can select before they reach checkout. These can include rates for shipment to Europe and the United States, or a facility for the customer to receive a quotation for postage and packing by e-mail.

Using your e-commerce site to generate some export sales is perhaps a first step. But it is not a planned or structured approach. It is only dabbling in exporting. If you really want to expand your business then you need to go into exporting in a professional way. My advice is to get professional advice. The governments of all major countries offer a range of services to support their exporters. If you are a UK exporter the place to get that advice is from your local contact at UK Trade & Investment. For similar advice and support an American exporter would contact the US Department of Commerce and International Trade and an Italian company would contact Istituto Nazionale per il Commercio Estero.

Assistance for exporters

The UK is still the sixth largest manufacturing economy in the world. According to the World Trade Organization, the UK was the tenth largest merchandise exporter (Figure 11.1) and the second largest exporter of commercial services (Figure 11.2) in 2009. So it is clear that exporting is very important to the UK, and the government actively encourages companies to export by providing expertise and a range of financial assistance packages.

FIGURE 11.1 Top ten merchandise exporters in 2009

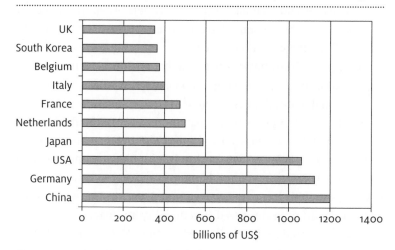

FIGURE 11.2 Top ten exporters of commercial services in 2009

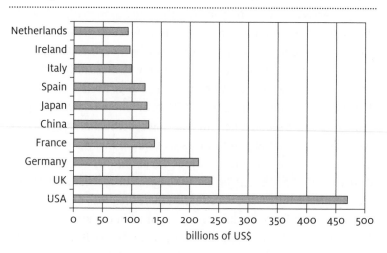

About 10 years ago the government established a new organiza-tion called UK Trade & Investment (UKTI) to assist UK exporters. UK Trade & Investment has developed a national export strategy that for the first time consolidates all government support for exporters under one organization, integrating the activities of the Department of Trade and Industry, the Foreign and Commonwealth Office, over-seas embassies and regional and local providers of export services in the UK. New arrangements have been established with Business Links and Chambers of Commerce.

According to information on their website, UK Trade & Investment has a staff of over 2,400 people in 96 countries with a network of international trade advisers (ITAs) in the UK regions.

In July 2010 the previously separate websites for 'trade', 'invest-ment' and 'defence and security' (the UKTI Defence and Security Organization – UKTI DSO works closely with industry and the MOD to promote UK equipment, products and services) were unified into one website with the new URL **www.ukti.gov.uk**. The site is now state of the art with improved functionality and navigation. There are also integrated social media feeds to the UKTI blog (with RSS to send you updates by e-mail), Twitter (if you join they will send you short, timely messages), Flickr (showing the UKTI photostream), YouTube (the UKTIWeb's channel with videos) and LinkedIn (you can join the UKTI group).

A vast array of information on exporting and export markets is avail-able on the UK Trade & Investment website (**www.ukti.gov.uk**). Inform-ation can also be accessed via Business Link (**www.businesslink.gov.uk**). I would recommend that you look at both websites. Although both sites cover many of the same subjects, the material and guides that you can download from the UKTI site are more related to export markets, market sectors, help in entering specific markets, making overseas visits, taking part in overseas exhibitions, trade missions, and so on. So typical guides include *Doing Business in France* and *Making the Most of Your Exhibition*. Although some of these subjects are covered on the Business Link site (and there are cross links between the sites), in addition Business Link has much more information on the 'nuts and bolts' of shipping your goods abroad. It has a wealth of information on things like export documentation requirements, customs regulations, VAT requirements, export insurance and the like, and typical guides that you can download include *International Paperwork: The Basics, International Transport and Distribution* and *Getting Paid when Selling Overseas*.

Note: In June 2010 the government announced that it will be abolishing the Regional Development Authorities, and with them, Business Links and that it will replace them with a number of Local Enterprise Partnerships (LEPs). The Regional Development Authorities will close by April 2012, by which time the Local Enterprise Partnerships will have been set up. The LEPs will provide the export support services that the Business Links currently provide.

New to exporting or already experienced?

Some companies are completely new to exporting, some have some experience and some are old hands. But all can benefit from expert advice and professional support services of the type offered by UKTI. Although some of the services (such as the 'Passport' scheme) are specifically designed for new or inexperienced exporters, others like the Overseas Market Introduction Scheme (OMIS) can be of use to new or experienced exporters alike for assistance in entering a specific overseas market. Virtually all of the UKTI programmes are personalized and specifically adapted to the requirements of individual businesses. I will cover the main services below, but I would mention that programmes on offer may vary and may be changed from time to time, and the financial support offered may be increased or cut, depending on changes in government spending. Also new web pages will be added and some will be withdrawn. Nevertheless, having used the services for many years, I can assure you that the general trend has been to continually improve the service available and if financial support is withdrawn from one area, it is usually soon reintroduced in another.

How to get started

We have said that exporting can extend your available markets, boost your turnover and avoid your having too great a dependence on your

UK-based customers. But moving into export is a large step for any business – so it's important that you honestly assess whether you are ready and able to take on the challenge.

UKTI Trade Teams are available in your local Business Link, and if you enter your postcode on the UKTI website it will bring up the name, contact telephone number and e-mail address of an international trade adviser in your nearest Business Link. You can then contact this adviser for specific information and guidance.

But before you contact an adviser, it is worthwhile downloading some basic information to read through, and even perhaps making an initial assessment yourself. If you go onto the Business Link website (**www.businesslink.gov.uk**) and go to the section 'International Trade', you will find a list of export topics beginning with 'Getting Started – Export Basics'. Under 'Export Basics' the first two topics are:

- Exporting – an overview. What's involved in selling goods or services to another country.
- Preparing to export. Assessing whether you are ready to export and planning your approach.

On both of these web pages you can access useful guides that you can print off or download as pdf files (although to do this you have to register).

The guide *Preparing to Export* again stresses that although exporting can be very rewarding and can boost your turnover and reduce your reliance on your UK-based customers, it is by no means an easy option. Developing new export markets takes time and money. There are many new challenges – from identifying the best markets and potential customers to making sure your product complies with local standards and regulations. Exporting isn't just an add-on to your existing business; it should be part of your overall business development strategy. Before you start exporting you need to prepare a complete export plan, which includes looking at all the costs and risks involved.

Bear in mind that:

- Exporting involves all the usual marketing challenges. You have to find customers and persuade them to buy from you. So you have to research the market in order to understand what the customers want and how the market operates – both may be different from what you have found in the UK.

- You will need to cope with extra logistical problems, paperwork and contractual issues. You will probably need to get standard contracts prepared for selling directly, through agents and through distributors. These contracts should be drawn up using internationally recognized terms and conditions and standard commercial practices, and make it clear what your responsibilities are.
- You will need to comply with regulations in both the UK and in your overseas markets. These may not be the same.
- You will need additional resources, both in terms of skilled personnel and financing. You will need additional personnel, but these people must also possess or learn the skills required in dealing with export markets. Payment terms will usually be longer than for your UK sales. Customers often want credit from the time they receive the goods. This could be weeks after you have produced and shipped the goods, so you get paid later than you would be by a UK customer. At the same time you may have to meet extra costs for transport and insurance.

With these additional costs, you may find that you just can't compete with local suppliers in some overseas markets. If the market only offers low margins or you don't have the extra resources that you need, you may decide that exporting is not for you. But if you have good products and efficient manufacturing, there will certainly be opportunities for you in overseas markets.

UKTI list 10 key steps to successful exporting:

- Research your market.
- Implement an export strategy.
- Construct an export plan.
- Choose your sales presence.
- Promote your product.
- Get the Customs side right.
- Get paid on time.

- Choose your distribution methods.
- Transport goods effectively.
- Have a good after-sales policy.

UKTI has a number of interactive assessment tools. These include a questionnaire that will help you recognize your strengths and isolate your weaknesses as you get ready to break into export markets. There is also a tool to allow you to identify export opportunities in any chosen market. UKTI's international trade advisers can provide you with professional advice on its range of services, including financial subsidies, export documentation, contacts in overseas markets, overseas visits, e-commerce, export training and market research. Support is available for companies of all sizes and with all levels of export experience, but schemes that offer financial support or grants are normally restricted to what UKTI defines as small and medium-sized enterprises (SMEs). These are independent companies with less than 250 employees, with an annual turnover not exceeding €50 million or an annual balance sheet total not exceeding €43 million.

Passport to Export

Also to be found on the website is information about UK Trade & Investment's assessment and skills-based programme, 'Passport', which provides new and inexperienced exporters with the training, planning and ongoing support that they need to succeed overseas. It offers a business health check, mentoring from one of their local export professionals, an individual export plan and a range of developmental training from which to choose.

Export Marketing Research Scheme (EMRS)

Before entering export markets you also need to assess the suitability of your product and decide which markets to try to enter. Again there is a wealth of country and sector information on the UK Trade & Investment website.

As we mentioned in Chapter 3, there is also a subsidized service that the British Chambers of Commerce administer on behalf of

UKTI. This service, the Export Marketing Research Scheme, helps companies carry out export marketing research on all major aspects of any export venture. This can include:

- market size and segmentation;
- regulations and legislation;
- customer needs, usage and attitudes;
- distribution channels;
- trends;
- competitor activity, strategy and performance.

Companies with fewer than 250 employees may be eligible for grants of up to 50 per cent of the agreed costs of export market research projects.

Overseas Market Introduction Service (OMIS)

UK Trade & Investment offers a service called the Overseas Market Introduction Service (OMIS), where for a competitive fee, you can commission research into a particular market. This can include preparation of a list of potential distributors in the country and even help in setting up meetings with them. OMIS uses the services of the UKTI trade teams located in the British embassies, high commissions and consulates across the world. Using their local staff means that you have access to their local language skills, market knowledge and commercial and political contacts.

Example

I used this service to find distribution in Austria. After providing the local trade adviser with a brief that included details of our company and our products, together with product literature and some material in the local language, I received a list of about 20 potential distributors. I narrowed this down to about six companies and the local trade adviser contacted them on my behalf. Four were interested and I set up a visit to the market to meet with them. The local trade adviser offered to set up the meetings, provide translation services and even allow use of the embassy facilities for meetings and presentations. The whole exercise took only about six months.

Tradeshow Access Programme

UK Trade & Investment also provides support for participants in overseas exhibitions and seminars. Participation is usually as part of a group, which is a big advantage for inexperienced businesses. The group is often on a UK stand, which is split into individual sub-stands for the participating companies. Grants are available to help SMEs with the cost of overseas exhibitions that are supported by the programme. To make sure that the grants are focused on companies that are new to exporting, there are restrictions on the number of times that a company can qualify for a grant. The grants payable can be £1,000, £1,400 or £1,800. The level is set for each show after discussion with the accredited trade organization (ATO) responsible for recruiting for the event. Most events are sector specific, so the Association of British Mining Equipment is the ATO for the International Mining and Machinery Exhibition in Kolkata, India, and the Engineering Industries Association is the ATO for METAL in Stuttgart, Germany, and METALEX in Bangkok, Thailand. Generally, the higher grant levels apply to selected shows outside Europe. Some major exhibitions such as the Hannover Fair or the IFAT exhibition (both in Germany) cover such a wide range of industries that they are not handled by one specific trade organization. Instead they are managed by the Birmingham Chamber of Commerce, which has a specific section that handles the support for a large number of exhibitions. These large exhibitions can have as many as 20 separate exhibition halls, and often each hall is specific to a particular type of equipment. So although there is still a UK section/stand on these exhibitions some companies decide that they need to be in a different sector-specific exhibition hall to attract visitors interested in their type of product. In such cases it is often possible for them to participate as solo companies and still qualify for grants.

Example

I have used the Tradeshow Access Programme on a number of occasions. When I participated in the Hannover Fair a few years ago everything was organized by the Birmingham Chamber of Commerce. Registering for the grant was easy, with the option of taking a part of the UK stand or booking our own stand. Because we needed to be in a different exhibition hall from the UK stand, we booked and built our own stand. But we were still kept informed of all the joint publicity events organized for the UK contingent and were able to use their stand facilities such as phone lines and meeting rooms. Although the grant only covered a small part of the cost of participation, the fact that we were getting that support made it much easier to get our budget for the exhibition approved by head office.

Sector-focused missions

Sector-focused trade missions last between three and eight days. Small businesses taking part in these trade missions are eligible for travel grants to cover up to half the cost of the visit. The missions are often specific to a particular industry or event. The process works in a similar way to exhibition support and is often managed by a Chamber of Commerce. They are an ideal way to visit a market that you are unfamiliar with and you can gain from the experience of the UKTI mission leader and others on the mission as well as from the local contacts that you make. I would strongly recommend a trade mission to make initial exploratory visits to countries such as Russia, Japan, China or Brazil.

Example

In 2004 I was looking for distribution in Russia, a country which I had never visited. There was an industry-specific exhibition taking place in October of that year in Moscow that looked to be an ideal place to meet possible distributors. When I contacted my international trade adviser she told me there was a planned trade mission to Moscow that coincided with the exhibition. A colleague and I were able to book onto the mission and we had four months to plan our trip. As part of the trade mission there were several briefing meetings at the offices of the Chamber of Commerce that was managing the trade mission. This was in the East Midlands and the mission was led by Russian specialist Tim Jelly, an international trade adviser who has been leading annual trade missions to Moscow for over a decade. At these briefings we were given a large amount of information about doing business in Russia and how to get the most out of our visit. We were also given a contact at the British Embassy in Moscow whom we could contact for information on anything relating to our visit. One thing that was made clear was that most people we would meet spoke only Russian, and that without some literature in Russian we would be wasting our time. At that time UK Trade & Industry had a service called the 'Subsidised Promotional Leaflet Service'. For the amazing price of £320 I was able to get 1,000 copies of a high-quality two-sided leaflet with one side in English and the other side in Russian. The leaflet included details of our company, our products and the applications that our products could be used for. The Russian translation was produced by a contact at the British Embassy in Moscow who liased with me to make sure that the translation was technically accurate. The embassy also provided us with a list of 30 potential distributors for the type of equipment that we wanted to sell in Russia. From this list we decided that there were eight companies who might be worth seeing. The embassy arranged meetings with these companies for when we would be in Moscow. Our hotel and flights had been booked through the mission organizers, but our contact at the embassy arranged everything else that we needed for our visit – safe transport from the airport, a car and driver to take us to our business meetings (and also to the exhibition) and an interpreter for the meetings. When we arrived in Moscow, the first day was spent at the embassy for detailed briefings on doing business in Russia and also on how to keep safe (important if it is your first visit). Subsequently all of those on the mission met up in the evenings, but during the day we all carried out our separate business meetings. The two-sided leaflet was of considerable help in giving our interpreter an understanding of our products so that she was able to make good, accurate translations. Our visit was a success thanks to the huge amount of assistance that we received from UKTI in the East Midlands and the local embassy staff in Moscow.

Other services for experienced exporters

Some of the UKTI services mentioned above, such as the Overseas Market Introduction Service and the Export Marketing Research Scheme, are of course used by experienced exporters as much as by newcomers. But there are some additional services offered by UKTI or the British Chambers of Commerce that are specifically aimed at helping experienced exporters to grow their business.

Gateway to Global Growth

This is UKTI's flagship package for experienced exporters. It is a free service that offers companies a strategic review, planning and support to help them grow their business overseas. The solutions suggested could be complex, and in some cases they may require services offered by other public and private sector companies as well as specific services offered by UKTI. They may require the acquisition of specialist information and skills, or guidance on how to achieve specific objectives.

Export Communications Review (ECR)

This service is offered by the British Chambers of Commerce to provide companies with impartial and objective advice on language and cultural issues to help them develop an effective communications strategy to improve their competitiveness in their existing and future export markets. It offers companies an on-site review of the way that they currently communicate with their export markets. Typically, this would include a review of the company's website and written materials and could also include meetings with the company's customers and agents/distributors. The reviews are carried out by accredited export communications consultants who have been trained in export communications by the British Chambers of Commerce. All ECR consultants are multi-skilled and have experience in exporting and international marketing. They will all have experience of living and working abroad and will speak at least one foreign language.

The Business Opportunities Service

The Business Opportunities Service is a free service providing sales leads that come via UKTI's global contacts network. Over 400 business opportunities are published each month. These may come from any industry sector in over 100 overseas markets. The leads range from market pointers to private sector opportunities, from multilateral aid agency tenders to public sector leads. Any UK company can register for this service on the UKTI website. When you receive a lead that is of interest, you can send a message back to the UKTI staff member who posted the opportunity. You can ask the UKTI staff member for more specific information on the opportunity if you need it and you will be sent the contact details for the company.

Springboard magazine

UK Trade & Investment publishes a magazine, *Springboard*, four times a year. This is free and you can apply to subscribe by calling 0800 298 3880 or by visiting **http://springboard.managemyaccount.co.uk**. *Springboard* includes news and updates on UKTI initiatives, features on export success stories, interviews with successful exporters and entrepreneurs, country focus articles and a directory of events.

In addition to government assistance, the independent company UK Exporters Ltd publishes the *British Exporters* CD ROM and all British Exporters are entitled to a full company profile on the database free of charge. Over 10,000 copies of the CD ROM are distributed each year worldwide. UK Exporters also publishes basic information on your company and its products on its website (**www.exportuk.co.uk**).

UK Exporters offers a range of subscription services that include an international press release service, an 'agents wanted' service and membership of the British Exporters Club, whereby subscribers can take advantage of discounted overseas travel, exhibitions, hotels, car hire, translation services and foreign exchange. The packages start at £195 for a year's subscription, which includes a company profile on the web database and can include product pictures and video.

Overseas markets

The measure of a country's wealth is its gross domestic product (GDP). Figures 11.3 and 11.4 show the International Monetary Fund's figures for GDP at market exchange rates for 2009 for major countries. It may come as a surprise to find that the GDP of Spain is as big as the GDP of the whole of Africa and about the same size as that of Brazil. The GDP of Brazil is more than 50 per cent of the GDP of the whole of South America.

FIGURE 11.3   GDP data for the top ten world economies

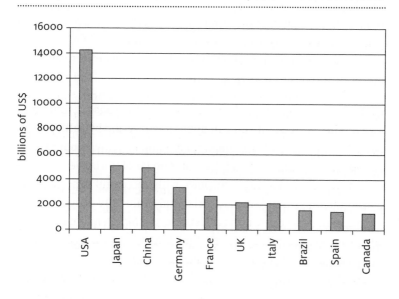

FIGURE 11.4   GDP data for next ten economies

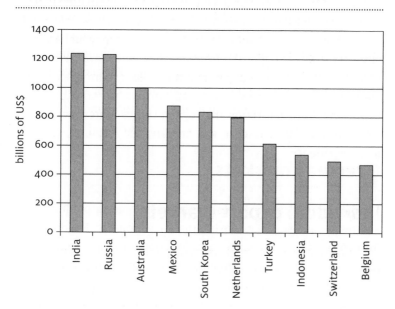

Which export markets should you consider first?

Depending on which definition you use, there are between 180 and 200 separate countries in the world. When you consider selling to export markets, it is important to consider the cost effectiveness of building up sales in one market rather than another. You need very good reasons for developing the African or South American markets before you develop your sales in Western Europe or the United States. But a country such as Norway, although only number 24 on the list, could be a very good choice for you if you sell equipment for the offshore oil and gas industry.

Different markets have different requirements and your products may require additional certification or modifications to be suitable for some regions, whereas they may be perfectly suitable as they are for others. Trying to export to a number of widely different markets can be expensive in both time and money. Most companies that are starting in exporting focus on one or two individual markets. In a large country like Germany or the United States, you may even decide to concentrate initially on one region.

I would recommend that you contact the international trade adviser at your local UK Trade & Investment, who will be able to help you decide on the most suitable market to try first for your particular product (details of regional offices and contacts are available on the UKTI website – **www.ukti.gov.uk**). Most new exporters start with markets that are relatively easy to deal with, such as other countries within the European Union (EU) or the United States. Developing countries are riskier to deal with and are best left until you have more experience.

Individual export markets

The approach to export markets is completely different from selling in your home market. Apart from distance, there are different cultures, different languages and different currencies to be dealt with. In most non-English-speaking countries, you should assume that business will be conducted in the local language.

A huge amount of information on individual countries is available on the website of UK Trade & Investment (**www.ukti.gov.uk**). For most countries this includes:

- a 'doing business guide';
- sector reports giving information on individual industry sectors in that country, including characteristics of the market, opportunities and key contacts within UKTI;
- FCO (Foreign Commonwealth Office) country updates. These are frequent assessments of political and economic issues relevant to business;
- overseas security information for business.

Maps, geographical and travel information on regions and individual countries can be found on **www.worldatlas.com**.

Some key points relating to major export markets are given below.

The European Union (EU)

The European Union (EU) has become the most powerful trading bloc in the world, with a population and a GDP larger than the United States (Figure 11.5). Britain now does more trade within the EU than with any other trading bloc.

FIGURE 11.5 GDP data for the European Union and the United States of America

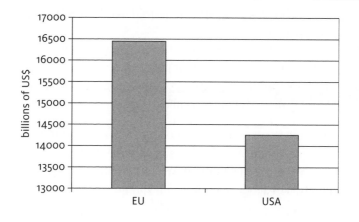

The EU has a population of over half a billion people in 27 countries, 16 of which belong to the euro area. The EU is now the 'home market' for every company operating within it. Companies based in England can sell directly to customers in Rome or Frankfurt, and French companies can bid for refuse-collection contracts in London. There are still some obstacles, but there is an ever-increasing move towards European rather than national standards throughout the EU.

Germany

- The largest economy in Europe, Germany has a population of over 81 million.
- The UK's largest European export market and the UK's number two export market worldwide (after the United States).
- Its trading practices are open and there is therefore competition from all over the world.
- It has a very wide industrial base, so it is extremely unlikely that any product will not face local competition.
- Key industries for exporters include vehicles and automotive components, aerospace, oil and gas, healthcare, IT, biotech and environmental engineering.
- Although there are many large German companies, the typical German company is small or medium sized – 99 per cent of all German companies are SMEs.
- Typical distribution would be based in Hamburg, Düsseldorf, Frankfurt, Stuttgart, Munich and Berlin.
- For most products, the German market is at least twice as large as the UK market.
- There is also potential to sell components to German companies that are exporting equipment or plant.
- To get into the German market you must be good at what you do, and to stay there you must be able to stay ahead technically.

France

- France is the largest country in Western Europe, with a population of about 64 million.

- The French and British economies are fairly similar in size.
- French industrial development has tended to favour the consumer goods industries and vehicle production. France also has well-developed defence and nuclear industries.
- France has nearly 30 per cent of the EU's usable farmland, and agriculture is a major industry.
- France is also the world's top tourist destination, with about 80 million visitors a year.
- Twenty per cent of the population live in Paris, which has assumed an economic and commercial importance greater than that of any other city in France.
- Paris is the centre of industry, banking, insurance and foreign trade, but if you want your product to be sold all over France your distributor needs to have branch offices in cities such as Lyon, Marseille, Bordeaux and Nantes.
- Since 2004 France has been developing what it calls '*pôles de compétitivité*' (competitiveness clusters). These include aerospace in Bordeaux and Toulouse, electronics and telecoms in Rennes and nanotechnology in Grenoble.
- France suffers (in the same way as the UK) from a narrow industrial base. This means that although in many industries there is stiff local competition, there are many gaps that offer potential for companies with the right type and quality of product.

Italy

- The GDP of Italy is about the same as that of the UK.
- It has a population of about 60 million.
- It has a good infrastructure and is a highly sophisticated market.
- Per capita incomes in the north of the country are among the highest in Europe.
- Due to the absence of raw materials, the Italian economy is reliant on manufacturing and the processing of goods.
- Key products are machinery, food products, vehicles, electrical appliances, packaging, textiles and clothing, building materials and ceramics.

- Italian industry is well known at home and abroad for the design and style of its products.
- Industry is concentrated in the large cities of the north, while the south of the country is predominantly agricultural.
- A distributor or local company should be set up in the north, where most industry is situated.
- Italy is home to a high number of trade exhibitions with global appeal. In 2015 Milan will host World Expo. This is an event on a world scale and will include many large infrastructure projects.
- The importance of Italy as an export market should not be underestimated.

The United States

- The United States is the world's largest economy and the GDP of just one state – California – would rank it in the top five nations of the world if it was a separate country.
- Current population is in excess of 310 million.
- The US economy encompasses every major industry and, since the US market is so large in itself, many US companies can make a perfectly good living without ever getting involved in exporting.
- Many US companies are only active in one state or one area of the United States.
- The sheer size of the United States and the cultural differences from region to region mean that it should really be treated as a series of regional markets with differing characteristics.
- Regional immigration patterns affect different areas. The fast-growing Hispanic population is becoming increasingly important in all US markets, particularly in the South and in California.
- In the United States very few products are sold directly to the end-user. They are usually sold through wholesalers, distributors or agents.
- You cannot deal with a company in New Jersey and assume that this company will be able to sell your product throughout the United States.

- If you choose to sell in the United States through a local company, you will probably find that this restricts your business to the geographical areas where this company is strong.
- Distributors in the United States tend to be successful in specific industries such as aerospace, chemicals, pulp and paper, water treatment. If your product is sold into two completely different industries, you would probably have to run two completely separate sets of distributors for these industries.
- You will probably need to get much of your product literature reprinted for the US market, because the United States uses the quarto format and not A4.
- You will need to get the material checked locally to make sure that it will be readily understood. (UK English and American English are not the same!)
- You need to check your literature to reduce product liability risks.
- You need to check that your UK trademarks and branding can be used in the United States and that your products comply with US standards and have any necessary US certification.

Japan

- Japan's economy is the third largest in the world after the United States and China.
- It is the UK's largest export market after Europe and the United States.
- It has a population of 127 million. Japan's consumers are highly educated, demand the highest standards and are early adopters.
- Contrary to popular belief, Japan is an open economy and there are no barriers to exporting to it if you have good-quality products that have something to offer.
- Japanese industry includes not only large, well-known companies with cutting edge technology supported by a large level of R&D spending but also far greater numbers of smaller companies.
- Prospects are good for companies manufacturing quality goods and components at reasonable prices.
- Japan is the world's largest manufacturer of motor vehicles and is a major force in semiconductors, electronic goods,

computer software and games, machine tools and industrial robots.

- Tokyo is the commercial and financial centre of Japan.
- The bulk of Japanese industry and population is situated in the coastal plain from Tokyo to Osaka.
- The pace of doing business in Japan is much slower than in the United States or Europe. Much store is placed on personal relationships and doing things in the proper manner.
- If you want to do business with Japan you need to understand Japanese business etiquette.
- The biggest barrier to trade in Japan is the complex distribution system and this is a problem for new Japanese companies as well as for exporters to Japan.
- To do anything in Japan you need a local presence – whether this is a distributor or a local company.
- The Japan External Trade Organization (Jetro – **www.jetro.go.jp**) has offices in most major industrialized countries to help promote imports to Japan.

The BRICs

The term BRIC was first used by Jim O'Neill of Goldman Sachs to encompass the rapidly expanding economies of Brazil, Russia, India and China. They are not a trading bloc, but they are the four largest economies outside the OECD (Organization for Economic Co-operation and Development). They are also the only developing economies with annual GDPs of over $1 trillion. By the second quarter of 2010 China's GDP had not only overtaken that of all individual European countries, but also that of Japan. A recent report by Goldman Sachs predicts that China's GDP will overtake the United States' by 2041. Over the same period it is expected that the Indian economy will overtake the European countries, putting it fourth in size to the United States, China and Japan by 2030.

Brazil

- Fifth largest country in the world – larger than the United States, Australia or the whole of Western Europe.

- A population of 185 million.
- Rapidly expanding middle class.
- Brazil accounts for more than 50 per cent of the GDP of the whole of South America.
- GDP per head is higher than either China or India.
- Key industries include oil & gas, advanced engineering, agriculture, environment, healthcare/biotech, pharmaceuticals, science, sports and leisure infrastructure.
- Ten-year energy plan with planned investments of over £150 billion in the first five years.
- Main business centre is São Paulo, but there are over a dozen other cities with populations of over a million.
- Brazil is a complex market and is for experienced exporters.

Russia

- The largest country in the world.
- A population of 142 million.
- Its GDP is about half that of the UK and it is the fourth-largest market in Europe.
- Russia possesses a wide range of mineral and energy resources.
- Key industries include oil and gas, aerospace, the automotive industry, engineering and pharmaceuticals.
- In the long term Russia is a market of great potential to exporters, but it is not an easy one to get into.
- Russia is a market for experienced exporters.

India

- A population of 1.21 billion people makes India the second most populous country in the world after China.
- More importantly, it has a middle-class population of about 300 million people.
- The Indian economy is now the second-fastest growing economy after China.
- It is projected that by 2030 the Indian economy will have overtaken all European countries, putting it fourth in size after the United States, China and Japan.

- The second-largest market for mobile phones after China, predicted to be in the top five vehicle producers by 2014, ranked third in the Asia-Pacific region based on the number of biotech companies in the country.
- India is a collection of linked markets rather than simply one large market. There are a number of distinct regions with linguistic and cultural differences, varying customer preferences and expectations and varying distribution requirements.
- Business opportunities exist in the traditional economic heartlands of Mumbai, Delhi and Bangalore but also in emerging cities such as Pune, Jaipur, Nagpur and Ahmedabad.
- English is widely spoken in business circles.
- India should not be ignored by experienced exporters.
- The UK India Business Council (UKIBC – **www.ukibc.com**) is the leading organization helping UK companies grow and develop their business in India.

China

- China's economy is now second only to the US economy in size.
- China is almost the same size as Europe, but has twice the population (1.35 billion people).
- A recent report by Goldman Sachs predicts that China's GDP will overtake that of the United States by 2041.
- China is the largest global producer of cameras, computers, textiles, toys and many other products.
- It is the world's largest consumer of iron, steel, coal and cement.
- It is not a single national market, but is made up of over 30 different provinces and municipalities.
- In addition to the well-known business centres of Beijing, Shanghai, Guangzhou and Shenzhen there are 270 cities with populations of over a million.
- Seventy per cent of the Chinese population live in the eastern part of China.
- Rapid and continuous industrialization and urbanization have created a vast and fast-growing consumer market.

- China offers huge export opportunities to large and small companies, but the complexity of the market and the speed at which it is changing mean that it is certainly a market for experienced exporters.
- The China–Britain Business Council (CBBC – **www.cbbc.org**) is the leading organization helping UK companies grow and develop their business in China.

Summary

- Exporting can help you to increase your potential market, increase your turnover, improve your business reputation and avoid your being over-dependent on sales in your home market.
- Academic research shows that exporting companies are more productive than non-exporters, achieve stronger financial performance and are more likely to stay in business.
- Exporting is very important to the UK and the government actively encourages companies to export by providing expertise and a range of financial assistance packages.
- UK Trade & Investment was set up by the government to assist UK exporters. UKTI has developed a national export strategy that consolidates all government support for exporters under one organization. New arrangements have been established with Business Links and Chambers of Commerce.
- Exporting involves all the usual marketing challenges. You have to find customers and persuade them to buy from you. But you will need to cope with extra logistical problems, paperwork and contractual issues and you will need additional resources, in terms both of skilled personnel and of financing.
- UK Trade & Industry have a large number of different programmes to support exporters, including the Passport to Export, the Export Marketing Research Scheme (EMRS), the Overseas Market Introduction Service (OMIS), the TradeShow Access Programme and sector-focused trade missions.

- For experienced exporters UKTI also offers the Gateway to Global Growth, an Export Communications Review (ECR) and the Business Opportunities Service, which is a free service providing sales leads through its global contacts network.
- A huge amount of information on individual countries is available on the UKTI website.
- When you consider selling to export markets, it is important to consider the cost effectiveness of building up sales in one market rather than another. Most companies starting in exporting focus on one or two individual markets.
- The BRICs (Brazil, Russia, India and China) all have economies of over $1 trillion that are rapidly expanding. Within the next 30 years China will become the world's largest economy.

Useful websites

Government statistics

www.ons.gov.uk – The Office of National Statistics – government statistics including economy, regional trends, consumer trends and Product Sales Reports (PRODCOM information).

www.thestationeryoffice.com – used to be government bookshop, now privatized, both online and with various branches around the country. Largest supplier of official publications.

Government support for exporters

www.ukti.gov.uk – government organization providing support for exporters including market reports, country reports and support for exhibitions, trade missions, etc.

www.businesslink.gov.uk – local support for business including export services. (Will change to Local Enterprise Partnerships in 2012).

www.export.org.uk – The Institute of Export – The UK Centre of Exporting Excellence.

www.britishchambers.org.uk/zones/export – British Chambers of Commerce export information.

www.iccwbo.org – International Chambers of Commerce.

Other useful sites for exporters

www.exportuk.co.uk – UK Exporters Ltd – publishers of British Exporters CD. Offer international press release service, agent finder service and membership of British Exporters Club.

www.competitivite.gouv.fr – information on French 'competitiveness clusters'.

www.jetro.go.jp – information on doing business in Japan.
www.cbbc.org – The China-Britain Business council.
www.ukibc.com – The UK India Business council.

Advertising and sales promotion

www.rab.co.uk – Radio Advertising Bureau.
www.oaa.org.uk – Outdoor Advertising Association.
www.iabuk.net – Internet Advertising Bureau.
www.payperclickuniverse.com – information on 'pay per click' advertising.
www.bpla.org.uk – British Association of Picture Libraries and Agencies.

Business ratio reports

www.the-list.co.uk – The Prospect Shop.

Direct mail

www.direct-marketing-lists.co.uk – UK's largest supplier of business and consumer mailing lists.

E-marketing

www.emailvision.co.uk – e-marketing.

Exhibitions and conferences

www.worldevents.com – event and conference management.
www.aeo.org.uk – Association of Event Organizers.
www.essa.uk.com – Event Supplier and Services Association.
www.aev.org.uk – Association of Event Venues.

Financial data

www.companieshouse.gov.uk – company accounts for UK companies.
www.dnb.co.uk – Dunn & Bradstreet – financial information on companies.

Information on local suppliers of services

www.approvedindex.co.uk – Approved Index – a local services online directory set up by Reed Business Information.
www.thomsonlocal.com – *Thomson Directories.*
www.yell.com – *Yellow Pages.*

Internet

www.nominet.org.uk – holder of UK domain names.
www.hostingreview.com – reviews of web hosting companies.

Market reports

www.ukti.gov.uk.
www.euromonitor.com.
www.frost.com – Frost & Sullivan.
www.keynote.co.uk.
www.eiu.com – Economist Intelligence Unit – Country Reports.

Market research organizations

www.mrs.org.uk – The Market Research Society.
www.esomar.org – Esomar (European Society for Opinion and Market Research).
www.caci.co.uk – Marketing solutions and information systems.
www.mintel.co.uk – Market intelligence for consumer goods.

www.britishchambers.org.uk/emrs – Government export marketing research scheme.

Public relations

www.cipr.co.uk – The Chartered Institute of Public Relations.
www.pcra.org.uk – The Public Relations Consultants Association.
www.pr.com – site for free posting of press releases.
www.uk.prweb.com, **www.prnewswire.co.uk** and
www.businesswire.com – press release distribution services.

Trade associations

www.taforum.org – Trade Association Forum – find trade associations in your industry.

Trade and local directories

www.kompass.co.uk.
www.kellysearch.com.
www.yell.com – *Yellow Pages*.
www.thomsonlocal.com – *Thomson Directories*.
www.wnii.co.uk – new products and services for manufacturing industry.

Other general sources

www.oecd.org – Organisation of Economic Cooperation and Development – GDP data and a wide range of statistics for OECD members.
www.eiu.com – Economist Intelligence Unit.
www.kompass.com – 'the business-to-business search engine'.
www.worldatlas.com – worldwide country information.
www.wikipedia.org – free online encyclopaedia.

Other useful websites

www.marketing-society.org.uk – The Marketing Society.
www.cim.co.uk – Chartered Institute of Marketing.
www.ismm.co.uk – Institute of Sales and Marketing Management.
www.ft.com – *Financial Times*.
www.iod.com – Institute of Directors.
www.ipo.gov.uk – The Intellectual Property Office – patents, trademarks, copyright.
www.uspto.gov – US Patent and Trademark Office.

Index